APPLYING FAMILY THEORY

Teaching, Research, Practice, Life

ANTHONY G. JAMES, JR.

Miami University

cognella®

SAN DIEGO

Bassim Hamadeh, CEO and Publisher
Amy Smith, Senior Project Editor
Abbey Hastings, Production Editor
Jess Estrella, Senior Graphic Designer
Kylie Bartolome, Licensing Specialist
Natalie Piccotti, Director of Marketing
Kassie Graves, Senior Vice President, Editorial

Printed in the United States of America.

cognella® | ACADEMIC PUBLISHING
320 South Cedros Ave., Ste. 400, Solana Beach, CA 92075

Brief Contents

Detailed Contents

Introduction

S o much, if not all, of what people do is based on theory and assumptions (Ford & Lerner, 1992). Consider the application of theory to at least one set of assumptions about families. If you are conducting family research, for example, you are most likely guided by some theoretical orientation about what should happen in families, how a family should look, what the preferred way a family should be is, and so on and so forth. The same can be said for family practice or clinical work. Though you may have been trained in a particular way of thinking about families, or you may work for a specific agency or institution that promotes a certain type of family dynamic or family structure, family theory is still likely to guide those practices. Additionally, in your daily life, whether this is your family of origin or your married family, you have a set of assumptions or some theory guiding the way you think about how a family should operate. What this text does is introduce family theory that has been tested in social science research to help a variety of professionals more effectively engage families.

This text is about the application of theory, family theory in particular. There are two overarching aims. First, this text aims to introduce a variety of family theories. Second, this text provides considerations for applying family theory across contexts. There are two overarching ways that the theory will be applied in this text. First, the theory can be applied in a professional capacity that includes engagement at some level with families. Some examples are research in the social sciences, teaching a class at a university, community-based programs for families, making policy decisions about families, and so on. The other way that family theory can be applied is simply in an informal setting, such as one's personal life. In either case, the thinking is that family theory provides some sort of valuable knowledge that promotes family well-being.

Why Considerations?

This text uses the language of "considerations" because there are very few universal absolutes about how to engage families. Also, families rely on a wealth of sources to guide the decisions they make in their daily lives or for their future. Sources can include traditions, superstitions, friends, observations, etc. Because family life is something that all humans experience, they are forced to choose a source to guide their family life. What family theory can do is provide some considerations to professionals who work with families (e.g., family scientists) or to families themselves that may better equip them with knowledge and skills that promote the achievement of their family goals. Much of this text is based on the idea that careful consideration of social science-informed and -based family theory gives people who are involved in family life better tools (i.e., theoretical tools) and options for making decisions in an informal context and/or about professional practice.

The Faynman technique is used in this text. Reyes et al. (2021, p. 1) describe it as "a mental model and learning strategy used to make complex information easier to understand."

Again, this text has two goals:

1. to teach the reader about family theory, and
2. to show how to use family theory in both professional and personal settings.

For the first goal, each family theory in this book will have a general over-view to help the reader know when to use it or, at the very least, under what circumstances it can be used in a way that assists families. The main goal is to give the reader the knowledge and skills they need to use family theory in context for the betterment of families. This text isn't meant to challenge or criticize existing family theories, or even to theorize about them, though this is part of what family scientists do (see Knapp, 2009). Instead, it aims to take complex phenomena and make family theory accessible to a wide range of people who interact with families on a regular basis, and to give them some ideas for how to do so in an informed way.

Developing Your Theory Toolkit

If you are reading this book, it is likely that you (or your instructor) thought it was important for you to know how to apply theory. If you are one of those who is looking for a competitive edge in social service marketplaces and desires to sharpen your theoretical knowledge and skills, I have a gift for you. The following is a list of family theory texts that I have used over the years and that have enriched my understanding and abilities as they relate to family theory. Each one is still part of my personal library, and I use them regularly. In fact, they helped me write this book! Don't be a professional who has books but no library. Having a personal library of the resources you need to give you an edge in the market is especially important.

I hope you'll think about adding them to your own library, not only to show your support for my wonderful colleagues but also because they give you more information about family theory that can help families learn and keep skills that make their lives better.

- *Family Theory Today: A Critical Intersectional Approach* (2nd ed.) by Allen and Henderson (2022)
  - ▷ I have used previous versions of this book for theory courses geared toward advanced undergraduates and early career graduate students. Their text provides a comprehensive overview of 12 family theories. Of note, the subtitle (*A Critical Intersectional Approach*), should alert you to the lens that the authors take in this text. Lastly, the illustrations are relevant in that they use contemporary challenges and issues families face to explain the theories.
- *Handbook of Family Theories: A Content-Based Approach* by Fine and Fincham (2013)
  - ▷ I have never used this book for a course, but I have used it for several writing projects. Their text organizes family theory based on subject or content areas of study in the field of family science (e.g., parenting, dating, conflict). For each content area, the text discusses how family theory has been applied to that subject area. This text is likely more appropriate for highly advanced undergraduate students or graduate students.
- *Exploring Family Theories* (2022) by Smith and Hamon[1]
  - ▷ This text is currently in its fifth edition. It provides a more comprehensive (e.g., historical roots, critiques) review (or exploration) of many of the theories covered in this text. One of my favorite aspects of the text is that it provides academic journal articles for each theory so that students may learn how the theory has been tested in social science research.
- *Readings in Family Theory* by Chibucos and Leite (2005)
  - ▷ A comprehensive collection of readings that provide an introduction to the field of family theory. The book covers a wide range of topics, including family systems theory, family dynamics, family life cycle, family communication, family roles, family structure, family decision-making, and family therapy.
- *Theory Construction and Model-Building Skills* by Jaccard and Jacoby (2019)
  - ▷ A comprehensive guide to developing and applying theory and model-building skills in the social sciences. The book provides an overview of the principles of theory construction and

---

1   Be mindful that the authorship order was reversed in earlier editions of the text.

model-building, and then explains how to apply them to real-world research problems. It covers topics such as the use of existing theories, the development of new theories, the design of models, and the evaluation of models.

- *Family Theory Sourcebooks*
  - ▷ If I were to query all of my colleagues, my hypothesis would be that the winner of the "holy grail of family theory" texts would be the family theory sourcebook series. This text is published by the National Council on Family Relations.
    - *Sourcebook of Family Theory & Research: A Contextual Approach* by Boss et al. (1993)
    - *Sourcebook of Family Theory & Research* by Bengtson et al. (2005)
    - *Sourcebook of Family Theory & Methodologies* by Adamsons et al. (2022)

As Jaccard and Jacoby (2019) explain, "Scientists formulate theories, test theories, accept or reject theories, modify theories, and use theories as guides to understanding and predicting events in the world about them" (p. 3). The theories about families in this text have been made, tested, accepted, rejected, changed, etc. Importantly, because these theories lay the foundation for thinking about policy and practice related to families, it is important that these theories are rigorously tested and modified to prevent higher-order consequences that harm people (Sowell, 2008). This text is meant to give some things to think about when applying theory in a way that helps a family work well. Before talking about the text's theories, it's important to review or explain some foundational concepts to help with effectively applying family theory.

Conceptualizing Context

The concept of context will be used quite frequently in this text. Context has at least two different meanings. One relates to the application of theory, and the other to human development.

For this text, both usages of the word *context* will generally refer to the setting where something is occurring. The application-related context refers to the setting in which the theory is being applied. For instance, scholars may use family theory in the context of their research to better understand family life. Practitioners can use theory in the context of their family-based programs as a rationale for implementing a certain technique to reach a particular programmatic outcome. Family theory may also be used in the context of informal family settings to improve decision-making so that decisions lead to the healthy functioning of the family. This is a simple example of how the context for applying theory can differ (e.g., research, practice, or informal).

Another way of thinking about context involves that of human development. Families in this text are those that are made through bonds with other people or animals (like pets; James, 2022). So, it's important to understand how context affects human development to understand family theory and how to use it.

Human development happens in the embodied contexts of people (like physical development), which are linked to other developmental contexts (like political, community, and social relationships, etc.; Overton & Lerner, 2014). Because the family context is a primary context for human development (Lerner et al., 2015), much discussion about family theory requires the use of context as it relates to human development.

Sources of Family Science Theory Content

The main sources for family theory content would be academic journals. This text uses a number of well-known family science journals, such as *Marriage & Family Review*, *Family Relations*, and *Journal of Family Theory & Review*. These are not the sole sources of family science theory. Far from it! But the point of this text is to give readers a general understanding of the theory and some ideas based on research for how to use the theory in real life.

The text was written with the idea in mind that the reader is someone who, currently or in the future, will work with families. So, the goal was to write the text in a way that lets the reader start building a professional portfolio of theoretical tools that can be used in settings where the practitioner is working with families.

There is no way to know exactly how many theories one should cover, nor is there a defined set of theories that catalogs some "official list" of family science theory. So, the theories in this book were chosen based on (1) a review of important journals, (2) comparisons with past and existing family science theory textbooks, (3) conversations with family science colleagues, and (4) an attempt to cover important family situations and contexts that family science professionals are likely to encounter in their work with families. Therefore, it is recommended that readers who work with families (or one day desire to) take the prudent step of being assertive and ambitious and ask family science faculty mentors, trainers, advisors, and colleagues for additional theories that can be included in one's toolkit. So, readers who work with families or want to work with families in the future should be assertive and ambitious and ask family science faculty mentors, trainers, advisors, and colleagues for more theories to add to their toolkits.

The Sidebars

I like sidebars when teaching. When writing, I use footnotes as my sidebar space. A lot. I think of these as "sidebars" that allow me to infuse an additional thought that would take me too far off the path of the book. So, footnotes it is. The footnotes allow me to provide a little extra information to students (win) and to send a special message to those scholars who are gracious enough to use this text in their course (win). That, according to the previous sentence, seems like a win-win.

Structure of Text

Except for the introduction, each theory chapter will start with the theory chart (see the next section). In the rest of the chapter, the information in the theory chart will be explained. At the end of the chapter, there will be a list of things to think about when applying the theory to a certain situation, as well as some general discussion questions about applying the theory.

Theory Chart

Basic premise	
Key figures	
Epistemology	
Assumptions	

Concepts	
Level of analysis	
Relevant studies	

This text will use the theory chart to introduce the key elements of theory. Each section gives the reader a chance to write down important information about the theory. This helps the reader understand the theory, which is important if they want to use it correctly. I regularly share this chart with my students so that they can build their portfolio of theoretical tools that can be used when engaging families.[2]

The purpose of this chart is to get students to understand what each theory is based on. Prior to starting discussions about theory, it is important to understand how each of these elements is linked to family theory.

> **Basic premise.** The basic premise of the theory can be described as the "elevator speech" about what the theory is about and/or used for. Each theory has one, and this can be used as a quick reference guide to aid the scholar or practitioner with the necessary knowledge of when or how to apply the theory.

> **Key figures.** Theorists work to create, support, and/or advance each theory. Knowing these people is important if you want to understand the theory and use it in different situations.

> **Epistemology.** There are many ways to build up theoretical knowledge, such as by having a lens or worldview. Scholars and practitioners can

---

2   I am a note-card person. Handwritten notes, specifically. Though I am not an expert on this topic, I tend to be biased toward the belief that handwritten notes are better at promoting student learning, relative to electronic notes (see Smoker et al., 2009), but it is in no way an absolute truth (see Aragón-Mendizábal et al., 2016). I encourage students to mimic this chart on a traditional 3 x 5 notecard.

use the theory correctly if they know how its content (read: knowledge) is put together.[3]

Concepts. Concepts in a theory are the elemental ideas or building blocks of the theory. There are usually many, and they can develop over time as scholars test new ideas related to the theory. Though I do not have *propositions*, I sometimes mention them when discussing theory. I like Smith and Hamon's (2022) definition of propositions, which is that they are the parts of a theory that hold together its different ideas.

Level of analysis. Family theories can focus on different levels of analysis. I don't know of a list of levels that everyone agrees on, but I usually pay attention to the following:

- Individual (the theory focuses on humans who are part of a family and how that human has a bidirectional relation with family structure or process)
- Family (the theory focuses on the family unit itself)
- Community (the theory focuses on families and their bidirectional relation with community factors, such as engagement with other families)
- State (the theory focuses on macrolevel processes in a definable state)
- Society (the theory focuses on the macrolevel of some defined geopolitical area)

Again, this is not a complete list, but it is important to understand the level of analysis to use family theory effectively.

Relevant studies. This section provides an opportunity to cite relevant studies that confirm or disprove aspects of the theory. It is recommended to add to the title something like "for African American families or Ohio families" when the theory chart is used for a specific program of research. This lets the scholars focus on family theory resources that are relevant to the specific topic area (see Fine and Fincham (2013) for examples of how many family theories can be used in a single area of family science).

---

3   I primarily teach advanced undergraduates and early career graduate students. There-fore, I only use a few categories of epistemology such as positivism and interpretivism. I recommend Sosa (2017) to students seeking to know more about epistemology.

Conclusion

There are a variety of reasons people may be interested in the scientific study of families. Two of the main reasons are that their job involves working with families (like a researcher or a practitioner) or that the person is part of more than one family system (like being married, having a family of origin, having social relationships, etc.). These two reasons alone make studying families quite interesting. However, one of the major challenges of studying families is that, because most (if not all) humans are embedded in some type of family system, it is likely that they already have a set of experiences and, thus, knowledge, about how families work or *should* work. Of course, this particular example means that a given person's experience and knowledge about families may be based solely on anecdotal evidence. Unfortunately, anecdotal evidence likely does not generalize or apply to all other families. This could make people think they know a lot about families but not be willing to learn about families that are different from their own. In fact, because of things like confirmation bias (Kappes et al., 2020) and conviction bias (Greene, 2018), a given individual may not even be open to hearing other perspectives about how families operate or function. To put it more simply, confirmation bias is the tendency or bias of people to look for information that backs up what they already want to believe. Or, not giving contradictory information the same importance or weight when looking for answers to a certain question or idea. So, what does this have to do with families?

The simple answer to the question in the previous sentence is that all people come from families of some sort. This provides humans with personal family experiences that become the norm, and it can be difficult for them to understand that there are other ways of *doing family* or even better ways of going about family life. Why? Since they probably have strong feelings about their own families, they are likely to look for information (or confirm their own beliefs about families) that backs up what they already think.

At the time this was written, there were about eight billion people on Earth. This means that there are billions of family systems and a lot of differences in how they work and what happens within them. Then, family scientists have to figure out how to study, understand, teach, etc., the many shared and different experiences that happen within and between family units. This text is mostly about the theories that scholars use to understand and work with families.

It is with these thoughts in mind that I state the following: If you are to really understand family theory and its applications, it is important for me to suggest that you briefly suspend some of the deeply held beliefs you have about families—just for a moment. Be open to differences from your own familial experiences and beliefs, such as

- understanding how families are structured and their diversity,
- understanding the diversity of processes that exist within families, and
- understand divergent perspectives, conclusions, and inferences made from data about families.

This is a brief list that can be expanded for quite some time. But that is not the point. The goal is to help the reader get the most out of this text so that families can learn together and equip the reader with a well-rounded set of tools to study and understand families—theoretical tools to better understand families and optimize opportunities to reach their full potential, whether we're talking about individuals within families, subsystems within families, or family units themselves. At the close of this text, you should have a good understanding of the theory used to study families.

The second goal of this text is to provide an example of how family theory is applied across contexts. Knowledge by itself is important. But being able to apply knowledge for the greater good of others is even better. As you read the text, add to your toolkit or professional portfolio so that you can make the most of your chances to use cutting-edge family theory to guide your family interactions.

Good luck! Let's get started.

References

Adamsons, K., Few-Demo, A. L., Proulx, C. M., & Roy, K. (2022). Family theories and methodologies: A dynamic approach. In K. Adamsons, A, L. Few-Demo, C. M. Proulx, & K. Roy (Eds.), *Sourcebook of family theories and methodologies: A dynamic approach* (pp. 3–20). Springer International Publishing.

Aragón-Mendizábal, E., Delgado-Casas, C., Navarro-Guzmán, J. I., Menacho-Jiménez, I., & Romero-Oliva, M. F. (2016). A comparative study of handwriting and computer typing in note-taking by university students. *Comunicar. Media Education Research Journal, 24*(2). https://www.scipedia.com/public/Aragon-Mendizabal_et_al_2016a

Allen, K. R., & Henderson, A. C. (2022). *Family theories today: A critical intersectional approach.* Cognella.

Boss, P., Doherty, W. J., LaRossa, R., Schumm, W. R., & Steinmetz, S. K. (Eds.). (1993). *Sourcebook of family theories and methods: A contextual approach.* Springer Science & Business Media.

Bengtson, V. L., Acock, A. C., Allen, K. R., Dilworth-Anderson, P., & Klein, D. M. (2005). *Sourcebook of family theory and research.* SAGE Publications.

Chibucos, T. R., Leite, R. W., & Weis, D. L. (Eds.). (2005). *Readings in family theory.* SAGE Publications.

Fine, M. A., & Fincham, F. D. (2013). *Handbook of family theories: A content-based approach.* Routledge.

Greene, R. (2018, Nov 13). *6 biases holding you back from rational thinking.* Medium. https://medium.com/the-mission/6-biases-holding-you-back-from-rational-thinking-f2eddd35fd0f

Jaccard, J., & Jacoby, J. (2019). *Theory construction and model-building skills: A practical guide for social scientists.* Guilford Publications.

James, A. G. (2022). *What is family science? An answer.* Prof_Ajames Enterprises Publications.

Kappes, A., Harvey, A. H., Lohrenz, T., Montague, P. R., & Sharot, T. (2020). Confirmation bias in the utilization of others' opinion strength. *Nature Neuroscience, 23*(1), 130–137.

Knapp, S. J. (2009). Critical theorizing: Enhancing theoretical rigor in family research. *Journal of Family Theory & Review, 1*(3), 133–145.

Lerner, R. M., Johnson, S. K., & Buckingham, M. H. (2015). Relational developmental systems-based theories and the study of children and families: Lerner and Spanier (1978) revisited. *Journal of Family Theory & Review, 7*(2), 83–104. https://doi.org/10.1111/jftr.12067

Overton, W. F., & Lerner, R. M. (2014). Fundamental concepts and methods in developmental science: A relational perspective. *Research in Human Development, 11*(1), 63–73. https://doi.org/10.1080/15427609.2014.881086

Reyes, E. P., Blanco, R. M. F. L., Doroon, D. R. L., Limana, J. L. B., & Torcende, A. M. A. (2021). Feynman technique as a heutagogical learning strategy for independent and remote learning. *Recoletos Multidisciplinary Research Journal, 9*(2), 1–13. https://doi.org/10.32871/rmrj2109.02.06

Smith, S., & Hamon, R. (2022). *Exploring family theories.* Oxford University Press.

Smoker, T. J., Murphy, C. E., & Rockwell, A. K. (2009, October). Comparing memory for handwriting versus typing. *Proceedings of the Human Factors and Ergonomics Society Annual Meeting, 53*(22), 1744–1747. https://doi.org/10.1177/154193120905302218

Sosa, E. (2017). *Epistemology.* Princeton University Press.

Sowell, T. (2008). *Applied economics: Thinking beyond stage one.* Hachette UK.

CHAPTER 1

Family Systems Theory

Basic premise	
Key figures	
Epistemology	
Assumptions	
Concepts	
Level of analysis	
Relevant studies	

Theory Overview

As per the goal of the text, this is a general overview of family systems theory. This overview is mostly about explaining the theory in a way that helps professionals (like family scientists) know how to work best with families. After the theory is explained, some considerations for practice are given that can be used in a variety of settings.

Family systems theory has a positive epistemology in that most of the literature on the theory states that family units are systems composed of interrelated parts.[1] The interrelated parts are the living organisms that make up the system. Though any given family is likely different from others or even itself in previous or future periods, this does not change the perspective that the family is a system. In this case, it is just a system that changes over time. One primary driver of change in family systems is change due to the development of one or more of the living organisms the system is composed of. For example, when an infant grows up and becomes a toddler, the tasks and responsibilities of both the child and the people in charge of caring for the child change. This changes how the family interacts with each other. Of course, expansions and contractions of family members also change the structure of family systems (more on this in the family development chapter).

A concise listing of family systems theory (FST) assumptions relevant to this text derives from Smith and Hamon (2022), Whitchurch and Constantine (1993), and White et al. (2015).

- Human family systems must be understood as a whole rather than by their component parts.
- Human family systems have the capacity to be self-reflexive, self-regulating, and goal-oriented.
- Human family systems are interconnected. Internally, between members making up the system and externally with other ecological entities.

The theory has been applied in many ways, though testing the theory is difficult because of the types of data that are needed to test its concepts. Given that, some considerations for applying this theory in context are discussed.

---

1   Depending on where you are in your training (e.g., bachelors vs. doctoral) or career (e.g., research scientist, practitioner), the epistemology of FST may not be of concern. It is beyond the scope of this text, but if you are interested, you can review the work of Simmons & Sutton (2019).

Basic Premise

FST grew out of the field of general system theory (Whitchurch & Constantine, 1993). *Merriam-Webster's* (n.d.) primary definition of "system" is listed as follows:

> *a regularly interacting or interdependent group of items forming a unified whole.*

Given this general definition of systems, FST uses the same approach to view the family. Specifically, FST views the family unit as an interconnected system (Cox & Payley, 1997, 2003). Returning to the *Merriam-Webster* definition, what is "regularly interacting" or the "interdependent group of items" in a family system would be the human and nonhuman members[2] elements serving as the individual parts that make up the whole unit, or the family unit.

It is crucial to note that the family system, which comprises the entire family unit, has some sort of connecting force or component. There are several forces or elements that can serve as the "binding agent" in family systems. Examples of binding agents (and an example of such a family unit) include the following:

- Legal (e.g., a single woman becomes the legal guardian of a child she adopts)
- Biological (e.g., a man and/or woman and their biological child)
- Social (e.g., best friends who are connected through shared meaningful events they've jointly enjoyed over many years)
- Etc.

There are an infinite number of examples of how human-based family units are connected. What is important for this text is that there is an understanding that families are made up of parts, and those parts are connected to each other given the family boundaries that make the family a unit distinct from other family units. Of course, the families are distinct not just in terms of boundaries but also in terms of characteristics (e.g., structure and process).

Key Figures

A brief listing of key figures or theorists in FST follows. A citation that directs readers to a source where they can find out more about the theories and their work follows each name. A second citation is for people who want to learn more about the theory and how to use it in real life, but don't just want to know the basics.

- Cybernetics
  - ▷ Norbert Wiener (1948, 1954)

---

2   I've said before (James, 2022) that human families must have at least one human member, but they can also have nonhuman members, like a pet.

- Family Therapy
  - ▷ Murray Bowen (1966)
  - ▷ Salvador Minuchin (1974)
  - ▷ David Olson (1988)
- Family Science Scholarship
  - ▷ Gail Whitchurch and Larry Constantine (1993)
  - ▷ Carlfred Broderick (1993)

Key Concepts

Several FST are presented here in hopes of aiding scholars and practitioners in applying the theory in context.

Interconnectivity. This concept advances the perspective that component parts of a system are interconnected within that system or family unit (Burr et al., 1979). This can mean that what happens in one component or area of the unit impacts what happens in other parts of the system. In this case, the unit is a family. Another way of thinking about this is to make it analogous to humans. Therefore, what happens to an individual member of the family in one part of the unit has a reverberating impact on other parts of the system. Many people use an infant child's mobile toy as an example of this assumption. When the baby touches one part of the toy, the other parts of the toy move in accordance with the force of the touch.

Wholeness. This means that the family unit is best understood as a whole rather than focusing on its specific parts (White, 1984). This concept can be described by thinking of the wheel system on a basic automobile. One way to explain this idea is to think of a basic car's wheel system. Let's assume the automobile is a sedan with four wheels. Each of those wheels is important in terms of safely moving the vehicle and its passengers. However, the car needs all four wheels to correctly drive its passengers from one point to the next. Each is important, but they must operate in unison to function correctly.

Bidirectionality. Families have an effect on the environment in which they live, and the environment in which they live also has an effect on them (Lerner et al., 2015).

Goal-oriented. Families are also goal-oriented entities (Broderick, 1993). Meaning, families pursue future conditions they desire to achieve. Some future conditions are based on rules or laws that are imposed on families (e.g., parents must adhere to compulsory educational policies in the United States), while others may be future conditions that are the sole desires of the family (e.g., children desire to eat meals with their parents on a regular basis or parents desire to take their children on one family vacation per year). Understanding the family's goals is important because it can help people outside the family understand what the family is doing.

Hierarchy. Family systems have hierarchical characteristics, meaning the members can rank higher, lower, or equal to other members in the system. Also, family hierarchy usually means how much power a family member has in a certain area of family life compared to the power of other family members (Whitchurch & Constantine, 1993). It is important to remember that hierarchical statuses in the family dynamically shift across time and space. Let's take the example of a Latinx immigrant family in the United States to further explore the space (or context) portion of this concept.

The Mexican immigrant family in the United States consists of a mother and father and their two biological children, one in preschool and one in fifth grade. Though the parents have power over the children in many ways, the older child serves as a language broker for the parent at school functions because the child's ability to speak English is more advanced than that of the parents (Buriel et al., 1998). So in the school context, the child has more power in the family system relative to the parents, even though they likely have less power in decisions such as when to do chores around the house.

Familial hierarchical structures can also dynamically shift over time. One simple way to show how time affects family life is to look at how the power balance between parents and children changes over time (Hagestad, 2017, pp. 405–434). Parents direct the lives of their children (i.e., those with higher power status) during the periods of infancy, childhood, adolescence, and early (and much of mid) adulthood. But as parents get older and lose the functional skills that make them independent, their more functionally able adult child starts to run their lives, making them less independent.[3] This change in family

---

3   Of note, it is possible for family units themselves to be hierarchically related to other family units. For example, consider the case of an extended family system where two parents have multiple sets of adult children who themselves have their own partners and children. In that particular extended family system, these family units can be set up in hierarchy with each other. Maybe adult child units live closer to the (grand)parents, which gives them more power. Or maybe the parents are emotionally closer to their adult children, which gives them more power. Or maybe the powerful career (hence more resources) gives them more power. See Whitchurch and Constantine (1993) for an extended discussion on the echelons of hierarchy.

power is the result of the integration of the changing physical and mental capabilities of both parents and their children and how those changes occur over time.

Feedback. Family systems are not static entities but dynamic living systems. The within (family members interacting with each other) and between (family member interactions with nonfamily members or other families) family interactions result in patterns of stability and change in the system. Family members have a choice, albeit constrained (James et al., 2018), in their response to the current state of the family system. The actions of family members either maintain stability in family states or processes or disrupt the current state of the family. The actions communicate feedback to the system. There are two types of feedback: positive (those that amplify change in the system) and negative ("dampens" change; White et al., 2015, p. 150).

Let's use an illustration of a family experiencing the death of a family member as a way to explain these concepts. In this example, the members of the family are sad due to the death of a loved one. When they gather for the ceremony to mark this occasion, many of the family members are solemn. One family member, realizing that the member who died would not approve of this type of emotional response, takes it upon themselves to cheer everyone up by recalling happier times they shared with the now-deceased family member. One by one, the mood begins to change in the family. This is an example of how positive feedback works in biological systems. In this case, the infusion of positive memories in the family was an amplifying force against the solemn mood. The family member's infusion of positive energy and emotion into the family setting amplified change against a solemn mood.

Cohesion. The concept of family cohesion refers to the level of emotional closeness between members of the family. Cohesion is a spectrum that goes from not being very close or emotionally connected (called "disengagement") to being too close (called "enmeshment") to each other. Each family has to determine what the optimal level of closeness may be for their given family unit, which would be referred to as being balanced. Olson (2000) discusses this concept at length when presenting his circumplex model.

Boundaries. Boundaries are the lines that show what is inside the family and what is outside of it. Boundaries can be rigid or permeable, which has implications for the well-being of the family. Again, you can read more about this idea in Olson's (2000) discussion of the circumplex model.

Family Rules. There are both articulated and unarticulated rules that govern families. For example, families may have unwritten rules about which chair each family member sits at during meal times. They may have unwritten rules about how the toilet paper should go on the dispenser (the loose end goes over the top or underneath the roll). Family rules may also be explicitly articulated such as chore assignments, frequency of attendance at religious functions, rules about social media usage, and how vacation options are chosen.

Family Roles. Families also have roles for each member of the family. Again, these may or may not be articulated, but each member has roles they perform to contribute to the functioning (or lack thereof) of the family.

Considerations for Application

The second aim of this book is to present readers with considerations for how to apply theory in context. Here we use a bioecological approach to show how the theory can be applied at multiple levels of context. Several examples are presented in the following section, exemplifying how FST can be applied in context.

Family Science Practice

Frey et al. (2016) discuss the historical practice of treating suicide as an individual-level process. But these authors say that a family perspective (like FST) can help with suicide prevention and intervention plans.

Holmes et al. (2013) looked at the couple's experience of becoming parents from the point of view of FST. They explore how variations in the family life experience of parents contributed to their either rocky or smooth transition to parenthood.

Johns et al. (2015) discuss how to teach systems-based theory in marriage and family programs using a journaling technique.

FST was used by Lindell and Campione-Barr (2017) in their paper about how family members change and stay the same as they move from adolescence to emerging adulthood. In particular, they focused on cohesion (how technology helps keep people together) and how the way people grow and change gives feedback to the system.

Olson et al. (2019) provide an overview of the circumplex model, which uses FST concepts to work with families in therapeutic contexts.

Weeland et al. (2021) use FST to develop a more nuanced understanding of the behavior-parent training literature, which gives a better understanding of which families the program helps or doesn't help, and why.

One approach family practitioners can use to better understand families and their dynamics is the genogram. Genograms are tools that can be made to show the structure and nature of relationships in a family system in a visual way (Silvestri, 2019).[4]

Family Science Research

Paley et al. (2013) used FST to investigate how military families experience multiple deployments. More specifically, how such repeated events affect family stability and change at each level of the family (individual, dyadic, and systemic).

Petren and Pulhman (2021) theorize about the importance of considering co-parenting and family routines in the context of managing family tasks. They argue that such an approach promotes family integrity and continuity.

With the growth of technology, scholars are curious about how that growth impacts family life. Padilla-Walker et al. (2012) used FST to investigate the relationship between family media use and family connections.

Applying FST in research and practice is an extensive topic in the family science literature. As shown in the following sections, family scientists have applied FST in a number of ways across many aspects of family life. The listing provides examples of how the theory has been applied in context to help guide and inspire future family scientists to engage families in a professional capacity.

One way to study families using the primary research method is to think of dyadic relationships as the lowest level of family research. If this is of interest to your work as a family scientist, Spanier's (1976) dyadic adjustment scale is a common tool used to measure dyadic relationships in family science.

Children

Dearing et al. (2008) applied FST in their study, which found that better parent-teacher relationships were linked with children's higher achievement in, and feelings about, school.

Pech et al. (2020) used the family system's theory to examine how having a previously incarcerated father impacts family dynamics. Interestingly, a strong co-parent alliance (between the mother and previously incarcerated father) was not significantly associated with children's behavior problems.

---

4   I cited this person because it is a *Psychology Today* article that has instructions for how to create a genogram and some example graphics. If you are not familiar with this practice or need to know more about it, this is a great resource for learning more about the tool.

Adolescents

Sang et al. (2014) found that parentification among low-income ethnic minority adolescent females was linked to lower engagement in sexual activities. Sample characteristics were composed of African American and Hispanic mother-daughter dyads.

Wang et al.'s (2021) meta-analysis examined whether family system theory intervention impacted family interactions among families with adolescents with type 1 diabetes. Findings revealed that FST interventions did help reduce family conflicts but no impact on improving self-management (e.g., glycemic control) of the medical condition.

Parent-Child Relationships

Lindell and Campione-Barr's (2017) study applied FST and found more improvements in the mother-youth relationship, compared to the more stable father-youth relationship, across the young person's transition from adolescence to emerging adulthood.

Adoption

Hunsley et al.'s (2021) qualitative exploratory study examined how the adoption process impacted children's relationships with other members of the family system. Findings revealed both positive and negative experiences, but also experiences that had impacts on the developmental trajectories (e.g., empathy, mental health, career choice) of the adopted children.

Marital Relationships

Pedersen's (2017) study used FST to examine how parental relational dynamics impact their satisfaction with their marriage. Results revealed that mother's *emotion work* and father's *perceived quality of child care by mothers* differed in the factors linked to their marital well-being.

FST is a major, if not the most important, theory in family science. One would be hard-pressed to find a family theory course that does not list it as critical to the understanding of families and family life. However, the FST concepts are difficult to test in research, which explains the lack of empirical examples that test FST-related hypotheses about the family. Retrospective qualitative data may be the best methodological approach to testing FST concepts given the currently available social science tools. This methodological issue does not reduce the importance of the theory. It has many practical applications that help professionals and/or families themselves. Thus, maintaining this theory in one's toolkit to engage families is of great benefit.

Conclusion

FST is a valuable framework for understanding the complex dynamics that occur within families (Cox & Paley, 2003). This theory emphasizes the interconnectedness of family members and the importance of examining the entire system rather than just individual components. By understanding the ways in which family members interact with one another, practitioners and researchers can gain a deeper understanding of the challenges that families face and develop more effective interventions.

When applying FST to research, it is important to use appropriate methods that allow for the examination of multiple levels of the system. This may include qualitative approaches that allow for in-depth exploration of family dynamics or quantitative approaches that examine patterns of interaction across multiple families. It is also important to consider the ethical implications of studying families, including issues related to informed consent and confidentiality.

In practice, FST can be applied in a variety of settings, including family therapy, couple therapy, and parent-child interventions (Becvar & Becvar, 2013; Minuchin, 1974; Walsh, 2003). By focusing on the family as a whole rather than individual family members, practitioners can help families to identify and change maladaptive patterns of interaction and promote healthy communication and problem-solving skills. Additionally, FST can be used to inform policies and programs that support families, such as those related to child welfare or mental health.

Overall, FST provides a useful framework for understanding the complexities of family dynamics and can inform both research and practice. By examining the entire system and considering the interactions between family members, practitioners and researchers can develop more effective interventions and policies that support healthy family functioning (Baptist & Hamon, 2022; Whitchurch & Constantine, 1993).

Discussion Questions

1. What are some ways that families are connected or bonded together within a family system?
2. Reflect on your own family system. What makes it a system? How is that system similar or different from other systems you are part of (e.g., friendships)?
3. Explain how cultural differences may result in variations in how hierarchy is expressed in family systems.
4. In what ways do family systems impact other systems in their environment? In what ways do external systems impact families?

References

Baptist, J., & Hamon, R. R. (2022). Family systems theory. In P. G. Boss, W. J. Doherty, R. LaRossa, W. R. Schumm, & S. K. Steinmetz (Eds.), *Sourcebook of family theories and methodologies: A dynamic approach* (pp. 209–226). Springer International Publishing.

Becvar, D. S., & Becvar, R. J. (2013). *Family therapy: A systemic integration* (8th ed.). Pearson.

Bowen, M. (1966). The use of family theory in clinical practice. *Comprehensive Psychiatry, 7*(5), 345–374.

Broderick, C. (1993). *Understanding family process.* SAGE Publications.

Buriel, R., Perez, W., De Ment, T. L., Chavez, D. V., & Moran, V. R. (1998). The relationship of language brokering to academic performance, biculturalism, and self-efficacy among Latino adolescents. *Hispanic Journal of Behavioral Sciences, 20*(3), 283–297. https://doi.org/10.1177/07399863980203001

Burr, W. R., Leigh, G., Day, R., & Constantine, J. (1979). Symbolic interaction and the family. In W. R. Burr, R. Hill, F. I. Nye, & I. Reiss (Eds.), *Contemporary theories about the family* (Vol. 2, pp. 42–111). Free Press.

Cox, M. J., & Paley, B. (1997). Families as systems. *Annual Review of Psychology, 48*(1), 243–267. https://doi.org/10.1146/annurev.psych.48.1.243

Cox, M. J., & Paley, B. (2003). Understanding family as systems. *Current Directions in Psychological Science, 12*(5), 193–196. https://doi.org/10.1111/1467-8721.01259

Dearing, E., Kreider, H., & Weiss, H. B. (2008). Increased family involvement in school predicts improved child–teacher relationships and feelings about schools for low-income children. *Marriage & Family Review, 43*(3–4), 226–254. https://doi.org/10.1080/01494920802072462

Frey, L. M., Hans, J. D., & Sanford, R. L. (2016). Where is family science in suicide prevention and intervention? Theoretical applications for a systemic perspective. *Journal of Family Theory & Review, 8*(4), 446–462. https://doi-org.proxy.lib.miamioh.edu/10.1111/jftr.12168

Hagestad, G. O. (2017). *Parenting across the life span.* Routledge.

Holmes, E. K., Sasaki, T., & Hazen, N. L. (2013). Smooth versus rocky transitions to parenthood: Family systems in developmental context. *Family Relations, 62*(5), 824–837. https://onlinelibrary.wiley.com/doi/10.1111/fare.12041

Hunsley, J. L., Ekas, N.V., & Crawley, R. D (2021). An exploratory study of the impact of adoption on adoptive siblings. *Journal of Child and Family Studies, 30*, 311–324. https://doi-org.proxy.lib.miamioh.edu/10.1007/s10826-020-01873-4

James, A. G. (2022). *"What is family science?": An answer.* Prof_Ajames Enterprises.

James, A. G., Coard, S. I., Fine, M. A., & Rudy, D. (2018). The central roles of race and racism in reframing family systems theory: A consideration of choice and time. *Journal of Family Theory & Review, 10*(2), 419–433. https://doi.org/10.1111/jftr.12262

Johns, P. A., Kreiger, R. L., & Hurff, C. M. (2015). "My life as a family therapist": A journaling method for teaching systems-based family therapy theories to undergraduates. *Family Science Review, 20* (3), 44–52. https://www.familyscienceassociation. org/wp-content/uploads/2021/07/2015-20-3-My-life-as-a-family-therapist-a-journaling-method-for-teaching-systems-based-family-therapy-JOHNS.pdf

Lerner, R. M., Johnson, S. K., & Buckingham, M. H. (2015). Relational developmental systems-based theories and the study of children and families: Lerner and Spanier (1978) revisited. *Journal of Family Theory & Review, 7*(2), 83–104. https://doi. org/10.1111/jftr.12067

Lindell, A. K., & Campione-Barr, N. (2017). Continuity and change in the family system across the transition from adolescence to emerging adulthood. *Marriage & Family Review, 53*(4), 388–416. https://doi.org/10.1080/01494929.2016.1184212

Minuchin, S. (1974). *Families and family therapy.* Harvard University Press.

Merriam-Webster (n.d.). System. In *Merriam-Wesbster.com dictionary.* Retrieved July 29, 2022, from https://www.merriam-webster.com/dictionary/system

Olson, D. H. (2000). Circumplex model of marital and family systems. *Journal of Family Therapy, 22*(2), 144–167. https://doi.org/10.1111/1467-6427.00144

Olson, D. H. (1988). Circumplex model of family systems: VIII. Family assessment and intervention. *Journal of Psychotherapy & the Family, 4*(1–2), 7–49.

Olson, D. H., Waldvogel, L., & Schlieff, M. (2019). Circumplex model of marital and family systems: An update. *Journal of Family Theory & Review, 11*(2), 199–211. https:// doi.org/10.1111/jftr.12331

Padilla-Walker, L. M., Coyne, S. M., & Fraser, A. M. (2012). Getting a high-speed family connection: Associations between family media use and family connection. *Family Relations, 61*(3), 426–440. https://onlinelibrary.wiley.com/ doi/10.1111/j.1741-3729.2012.00710.x

Paley, B., Lester, P., & Mogil, C. (2013). Family systems and ecological perspectives on the impact of deployment on military families. *Clinical Child and Family Psychology Review, 16*, 245–265. https://doi.org/10.1007/s10567-013-0138-y

Pech, A., Curran, M., Speirs, K., Li, X., Barnett, M., & Paschall, K. (2020). Understanding child behavior problems in young children with previously incarcerated fathers: Parents' depressive symptoms, relationship quality, and coparenting. *Marriage & Family Review, 56*(6), 553–574. https://doi.org/10.1080/01494929.2020.1728602

Pedersen, D. E. (2017). Quantity and quality: A more nuanced look at the association between family work and marital well-being. *Marriage & Family Review, 53*(3), 281–306. https://doi.org/10.1080/01494929.2016.1177632

Petren, R. E., & Puhlman, D. J. (2021). Routines and coparenting as interrelated family management systems. *Journal of Family Theory & Review, 13*(2), 164–180. https:// doi.org/10.1111/jftr.12422

Sang, J., Cederbaum, J. A., & Hurlburt, M. S. (2014). Parentification, substance use, and sex among adolescent daughters from ethnic minority families: The moderating role of monitoring. *Family Process, 53*, 252–266. https://doi.org/10.1111/famp.12038

Silvestri, K. (2019, June 30). Who do you think think you are? Clues from your family of origin. *Psychology Today.* https://www.psychologytoday.com/us/blog/wider-lens/201906/who-do-you-think-you-are

Simmons, B., & Sutton, J. (2019). Epistemology in family systems theory. In J. Lebow, A. Chambers, & D. Breunlin (Eds.), *Encyclopedia of couple and family therapy* (pp. 915–923). Springer.

Spanier, G. B. (1976). Measuring dyadic adjustment: New scales for assessing the quality of marriage and similar dyads. *Journal of Marriage and the Family, 38*(1), 15–28. https://doi.org/10.2307/350547

Walsh, F. (2003). Family resilience: A framework for clinical practice. *Family Process, 55*(4), 639–653. https://doi.org/10.1111/j.1545-5300.2003.00001.x

Wang, H., Guo, J., Guo, Y., Lv, W., Jiang, Y., & Whittemore, R. (2021). Effectiveness of Family Systems Theory Interventions on Adolescents with Type 1 Diabetes: A Meta-analysis. *Journal of Child and Family Studies,* 1–13. https://doi.org/10.1007/s10826-021-02069-0

Weeland, J., Helmerhorst, K. O., & Lucassen, N. (2021). Understanding differential effectiveness of behavioral parent training from a family systems perspective: Families are greater than "some of their parts." *Journal of Family Theory & Review, 13*(1), 34–57. https://doi.org/10.1111/jftr.12408

Whitchurch, G. G., & Constantine, L. L. (1993). Systems theory. In P. G. Boss, W. J. Doherty, R. LaRossa, W. R. Schumm, & S. K. Steinmetz (Eds.), *Sourcebook of family theories and methods: A contextual approach* (pp. 325–355). Plenum Press. https://doi.org/10.1007/978-0-387-85764-0_14

White, J. M. (1984). Not the sum of its parts. *Journal of Family Issues, 5,* 515–518. https://journals.sagepub.com/doi/pdf/10.1177/019251384005004007

White, J. M., Martin, T. F., & Adamsons, K. (2015). *Family theories: An introduction.* SAGE Publications.

Wiener, N. (1948). *Cybernetics or control and communication in the animal and the machine.* The Technology Press/Wiley.

Wiener, N. (1954). *The human use of human beings.* New York.

CHAPTER 2

Family Development Theory

Basic premise	
Key figures	
Epistemology	
Assumptions	
Concepts	
Level of analysis	
Relevant studies	

Theory Overview

As per the goal of the text outlined in the preface, this is a general overview of family development theory. This overview focuses on explaining the theory in a way that helps professionals who work with families, like family scientists, do their jobs better. Following the presentation of the theory, some considerations for practice are provided to assist with the application of the theory across a variety of contexts.

The theory uses both positivist and interpretive worldviews, with several assumptions. Family development theory can be applied in context at multiple levels because family development theory can be used to examine individual change within the context of families, relational change within the context of families, or family change itself. For each, time is a necessary factor in the changes that occur within family life (e.g., contraction and expansion).

Several scholars have listed out assumptions of family development theory. Specifically, Aldous (1978), Allen and Henderson (2017), Mattessich and Hill (1987, pp. 437–469), Rodgers and White (2009, pp. 225–257), and Smith and Hamon (2022) are the sources of the assumptions described in this chapter. Of note, White (1991) and Chibucos et al. (2005) were also consulted, but those particular sources discussed the development of families as a derivative of life course theory (e.g., family life course theory and life course development framework).

- Family behavior is influenced by the family's past and future goals.
- Individuals and families change over time in relatively consistent patterns in alignment with the norms of the contexts in which they are embedded.
- The development of individual family members and the family unit itself is influenced by bidirectional relationships.
- Individuals and families have tasks for each family stage that are based on the norms of the contexts in which they are embedded.

Basic Premise

The value and skill that can be used as a result of learning family development theory is an understanding of the ways that families change over time. That change can be in terms of family structure or their processes. But first, it is important for the practitioner to first clarify their own definition of the concept of family. Prior to application of the theory, the practitioner should take inventory of the way they define family. Then, the practitioner should develop a way to determine how the families they seek to engage actually define the concept of family. If the goal is to engage families in a healthy and productive manner, how well their and their clients (i.e., family) define the concept of family will likely impact the course of engagement between the practitioner and the family.

Another important consideration for engaging families using family development theory is that families may be in more than one phase or stage at a given time. The way that family development theory has been used in the past, it does not always allow for complexity in family life. Including a way to understand how families and/or their members can be in multiple stages (or even multiple families) at the same time adds richness to the practitioner's ability to fully understand the family they are engaging and assist them with what the family desires to be assisted with.

Key Figures

A brief listing of key figures or theorists of family development theory follows. Each name is followed by a citation that points to a source where more information can be learned about the theories and their work. The latter is for those looking to increase their understanding of the theory for reasons beyond a basic understanding of the theory and how to apply it in context.

- Joan Aldous (1978, 1990)
  - ▷ *Family Careers: Developmental Change in Families*
  - ▷ *Family Development and the Life Course: Two Perspectives on Family Change*
- Reuben Hill (1986)
  - ▷ *Life Cycle Stages for Types of Single Parent Families: Of Family Development Theory*
- Evelyn Duvall (1957, 1972, 1988)
  - ▷ *Family Development,*
  - ▷ *Family Development Applications: An Essay Review,* and
  - ▷ *Family Development's First Forty Years,* respectively
- Todd Martin (2018)
  - ▷ *Family Development Theory 30 Years Later*
- James White (1991)
  - ▷ *Dynamics of Family Development: A Theoretical Perspective*
- Roy Rodgers (1964)
  - ▷ *Toward a Theory of Family Development*

Key Concepts

- Family Development
  - ▷ Families change over time. This can be in terms of their structure or in terms of their processes related to being in a given family stage.

- Time and Timing
  - ▷ Time is the force that brings about various changes to family life, whether its structure or process.
  - ▷ Timing refers to the period at which families enter, pass through, or exit given stages or experiences compared to expectations of the family based on social norms.[1]

- Family Stages
  - ▷ Families experience distinct periods of family life that are qualitatively different from past or future periods. These periods are called stages in this theory, and families can different in terms of their structure or their interactions. There is not one set of defined stages that all families experience; rather, the stages that families experience will depend on the context in which the family is embedded. The transition from one period to the next is likely due to structural changes to the family, which brings about changes in the tasks relevant to the new stage. Some broadly defined examples of stages families may experience include: introduction of children into the family, stage of caring for infants, stage of preparing young children for school, stage of children transitioning to different developmental periods (e.g., adolescence) and to different school levels, stage of children moving out of the home, stage of parents reconnecting with each other as their children leave the home, stage of adult children finding partners and starting their own families, etc. What stages families experience will vary from one place to the next, or from even one cultural group to the next. Families have many developmental pathways, impacting the sequence of stages their families enter into, through, and out of.

- Family Tasks
  - ▷ Within each development stage that families experience, there are task expectations related to being in that given family stage. A family in the stage that includes a newborn child is expected to pour many resources into the survival and thriving of that newborn child because that child cannot survive or thrive without the help of their family.

- Social Norms
  - ▷ Social norms related to family development theory consider how families are defined, the stages families experience, task

---

1   Some families may experience having their first child when the couple is in their early 20s, while other couples may have their first child in their early 30s. This 10 year difference impacts the development of each family, especially based on social norms.

expectations within stages, etc., which are all dependent on the social norms of the geographic location in which the family is embedded.

Consideration for Application

One approach to applying family development theory is through the various levels of analyzing families. We'll use Bronfenbrenner's (1979) concentric circles as a guide representing spheres of influence on individual development. The levels are macro (society level), exo (indirect effects), mezzo (combined effects of multiple micro factors), micro (direct effects). Chronolevel effects are also considered, though this component of the theory was introduced later than the other levels (Bronfenbrenner & Morris, 1998; Tudge et al., 2009).

Chrono
Chronolevel effects consider the impact of time on families. Of course, time is a major concept in family development theory. The fact that there are multiple stages (and tasks within each stage) that families progress through happens because time elapses. As time passes or elapses, families experience transitions through various family stages or careers, which adjusts the tasks the family and its individual members are responsible for in the new stage it has transitioned to.

Macro
Family development theory can also be examined at the macrolevel. For instance, some entities (e.g., policymakers, social service agency management) are interested in family change at the macro level, because they make decisions based on macrolevel changes in family life. For instance, the State of Families Project uses a double entendre to understand families, both the conditional state as well as the state in terms of the geographic location of families. The goal of the State of Families Project is to produce consistent content updates on the conditional state of families in a specific geographic location. Such content will allow decision-makers to better understand how time impacts macrolevel family conditions in a specified area. The inaugural paper in this series by Wilkins et al. (2023) focused on the challenges and strengths facing Ohio families.

Exo
Exolevel influence on families considers indirect effects. For example, the friends and/or acquaintances of a given individual family member can have

profound effects on either the structure or dynamics of a family unit. Let's consider a scenario of a mom (Pat) of a given family who is friends with a woman (Jill) who is very goal oriented about her health. Though Jill never interacts with the other members of Pat's family, she has a great impact on the whole family unit through her interactions with Jill. Jill's health-conscious lifestyle may influence Pat to start serving different types of food, or encourage family walks after dinner, or start meal prepping for the week to ensure the consumption of healthy foods, etc. In each case, Jill represents an exolevel (or indirect) influence on Pat's family because the only member of the family Jill directly interacted with was Pat, even though that interaction then had subsequent effects on the family's health-related activities.

Mezzo

Mezzo-level effects on families consider the combined effect of two microlevel effects. Consider the example of a family of two gay men, their adopted child, and their shared biological child.[2] The family resides in a state that has not been very welcoming to same-sex families, yet the family was able to identify a community that was welcoming and loving toward their family but even valued and added to the diversity the family brought to their community. Though the family experiences many fears about potential policies or interactions that negatively impact members of the family or the family as a whole, having found a loving and welcoming community has been beneficial for the family member's mental health and ability to live their lives how they see fit, and in a community that values their family. Each sphere of influence (living in a state inhospitable to same-sex families AND living in a community that loves and values their family) combines the impact of influence it has on the well-being and daily functioning of their family.

Micro

Microsystem effects on families consider the direct impacts on family life. There are many direct impacts on family life that can impact the structure of, and processes within, family life. Some simple examples include the community that the family resides in (e.g., rural vs. urban), the religious faith of the community (e.g., whether it is a faith that believes in contraception or not), the friendships of each family member, within-familial multigenerational effects (e.g., how grandmothers use of family narratives directly influence

---

2   The two men had an agreement with a female friend where a child was reproduced via the sperm of one of the men and the eggs of the female friend. Though the child is technically only biologically related to one of the men, they agreed that they would socially consider the child as their biological child.

the identity development of adolescents; Taylor et al., 2013), social policies available to families, etc. All of these variables can have a direct impact on families in terms of how they expand and contract (Smith & Hamon, 2022), or the dynamics and processes occurring within the family.

There are several additional considerations that are important to the application of family development theory. I focus on three examples here: using the language of structure and process in practice with families, that families can be in multiple stages or phases at a given time, and changes can be positive or negative.

Changes in Structure and Process

There are at least two broad ways of approaching ways that family development theory can be applied to the change in families over time. One approach is their structure, with the other being the patterns of interactions occurring within a given family.

Structure refers to what the family is composed of that gives them an identity (e.g., nuclear family, LGBTQ+ family, single parent family, step or blended or repartnered family). Family development theory would focus on how the family structure changed over time. Duvall labeled these changes as expansions and contractions. There are several different ways families expand (e.g., birth of a new child, family adopts a child, a parent gets remarried after divorce) or contract (e.g., a family member dies, a family member goes off to college and lives on campus, an adult child marries and starts their own family).

Family development theory is not just about the structure of families that categorizes them into a given stage or phase typically expected in the normative context the family is embedded in, but also about the tasks or responsibilities that align with the given stage the family is in. Those tasks for a given stage can be imagined as the patterns of interaction of the family, to meet the goals or responsibilities of the given stage. As families change stages, the patterns of interaction also change. Families engage in all sorts of patterns of interactions (e.g., behaviors, rituals, actions) that signify they are bonded together in a meaningful way that makes them a family (James, 2022). Assuming the family lives in the same household, patterns of interaction can include the typical time the family unit eats its daily dinner meals, or the rhythm at which the family eats the meal in unison is another type of family dynamic (Fiese, 2006). Additional patterns of interaction can include the manner in which the family shares resources and tasks related to caring for the well-being of other family members. As members of the family age, each of these examples can shift because new developmental stages bring about different tasks the family is required to meet, according to social norms (Smith & Hamon, 2022).

Positive or Negative Change

Change in family development theory is neutral in terms of whether the change is positive (beneficial) or negative (harmful) for the family or both. Each change that the family experiences can present a wealth of interpretations regarding whether the change is beneficial or harmful. In each phase of family development theory, regardless of which set of stages is being used or the geographic context, it is likely that some element of both promises and/or challenges is present for the family. For instance, it takes many resources to care for an infant. For many couples, the news of pregnancy brings excitement and joy. However, it is also the case that most couples experience a decrease in relationship satisfaction (Kuile et al., 2021), likely due to the vast amount of resources dedicated to caring for a newborn child. In the course of a year, the pending and actual expansion of the family brings both positive and negative emotions to the family, which likely impacts their interaction with each other. Of course, many couples successfully navigate this stage and move on to subsequent stages and responsibilities the family will experience. For either, it can be positive or negative. The point of consideration here is to simply encourage scholars to engage families with an open mind about whether and how they interpret the family change in terms of whether the change is positive or negative.

Multiple Phases at Once

It is common to consider the application of family development theory to families and only consider their being in one given stage of development at a given time. Depending on the family, this may very well be true. For instance, a nuclear family that is stable may transition through the various stages and tasks in a sequential manner much like the ideals of family prevalent in society (Levin, 2020, pp. 123–133). However, many have written about the complexity and diversity of families (Coontz, 2016; Letiecq, 2019), which would suggest that not all families traverse through the stages in the purported sequential order. In fact, our same nuclear family may decide to have a child 10–15 years after their first child, which could mean they may "launch" family members into college (age 19) and primary school (age 5) at the same time. More complexity may include families where adults have children with multiple partners, at the same or different time points, further nuancing what stage a given family member (or the family as a whole) may be in at a given time. The point is not to provide an exhaustive list of scenarios but rather to point to the complexity of determining what "stage" a family may be in by encouraging family practitioners to be prepared to make plural stage to "stages" for some families they may engage.

Conclusion

Family development theory's main criticism shouldn't be that it's outmoded, but that it doesn't incorporate enough family structures (Laszloffy, 2004). Most are predicated on having children. This affects childless couples' family life cycles, careers, and patterns. They can certainly fulfill some traditional roles that provide them family careers in adjacent family units (e.g., even though they don't have kids, each member of the couple may still be an uncle, aunt, nephew, niece), but they likely have a different life cycle than family units that bear children.

Discussion Questions

1. Explain how the concept of time is essential to family development theory.
2. Provide a critique of using family development theory in a way that purports families are only in one stage of development at a given time.
3. What role do social norms play in the tasks assigned to families for a given family stage of development?
4. Provide an example that articulates how family development is neutral in whether family transitions are positive or negative.

References

Aldous, J. (1978). *Family careers: Developmental change in families.* Wiley.

Aldous, J. (1990). Family development and the life course: Two perspectives on family change. *Journal of Marriage and the Family, 52*(3), 571–583.

Allen, K. R., & Henderson, A. C. (2017). *Family theories: Foundations and applications.* John Wiley & Sons.

Bronfenbrenner, U. (1979). *The ecology of human development: Experiments in nature and design.* Harvard University Press.

Bronfenbrenner, U., & Morris, P. A. (1998). The ecology of developmental processes. In W. Damon & R. M. Lerner (Eds.), *Handbook of child psychology: Theoretical models of human development* (Vol. 1, 5th ed., pp. 993–1023). Wiley.

Chibucos, T. R., Leite, R. W., & Weis, D. L. (Eds.). (2005). *Readings in family theory.* Sage.

Coontz, S. (2016). *The way we never were: American families and the nostalgia trap.* Hachette UK.

Duvall, E. M. (1957). *Family development.* Lippincott.

Duvall, E. M. (1972). Family development applications: An essay review. *The Family Coordinator, 21*(3), 331–333. https://doi.org/10.2307/582879

Duvall, E. M. (1988). Family development's first forty years. *Family Relations, 37*(2), 127–134.

Fiese, B. H. (2006). *Family routine and rituals.* Yale.

Hill, R. (1986). Life cycle stages for types of single parent families: Of family development theory. *Family Relations,* 35(1), 19–29. https://doi.org/10.2307/584278

James, A. G. (2022). "What is family science?": *An answer.* Prof_Ajames Enterprises.

Kuile, H. t., van der Lippe, T., & Kluwer, E. S. (2021). Relational processes as predictors of relationship satisfaction trajectories across the transition to parenthood. *Family Relations, 70*(4), 1238–1252. https://doi.org/10.1111/fare.12546

Laszloffy, T. A. (2002). Rethinking family development theory: Teaching with the systemic family development (SFD) model. *Family Relations, 51*(3), 206–214.

Letiecq, B. L. (2019). Surfacing family privilege and supremacy in family science: Toward justice for all. *Journal of Family Theory & Review, 11*(3), 398–411. https://doi.org/10.1111/jftr.12338

Levin, I. (2020). *Stepfamilies: History, research, and policy.* Routledge.

Martin, T. F. (2018). Family development theory 30 years later. *Journal of Family Theory & Review, 10*(1), 49–69. https://doi.org/10.1111/j.1741-3729.2002.206098.x

Mattessich, P., & Hill, R. (1987). *Handbook of marriage and the family.* Springer.

Rodgers, R. H. (1964). Toward a theory of family development. *Journal of Marriage and the Family, 26*(3), 262–270. https://doi.org/10.2307/349456

Rodgers, R. H., & White, J. M. (2009). Family development theory. In Boss et al. (Eds.), *Sourcebook of family theories and methods* (pp. 225–273). Springer.

Smith, S. R., & Hamon, R. R. (2022). *Exploring family theories* (5th Ed). Oxford University Press.

Taylor, A. C., Fisackerly, B. L., Mauren, E. R., & Taylor, K. D. (2013). "Grandma, tell me another story": Family narratives and their impact on young adult development. *Marriage & Family Review, 49*(5), 367–390. https://doi.org/10.1080/01494929.2012.762450

Tudge, J. R., Mokrova, I., Hatfield, B. E., & Karnik, R. B. (2009). Uses and misuses of Bronfenbrenner's bioecological theory of human development. *Journal of Family Theory & Review, 1*(4), 198–210. https://doi-org.proxy.lib.miamioh.edu/10.1111/j.1756-2589.2009.00026.x

White, J. M. (1991). *Dynamics of family development: A theoretical perspective.* Guilford Press.

Wilkins, J. K., Bates, J. S., Betz, M. R., Civittolo, D. J., Fox, J., Jones, L. E, Porfeli, E. J., Powers-Barker, P. K., Reister, H. L., Remley, D. T., & Wapner, A. (2023). The 2022 state of Ohio families: Challenges and Promises. *Marriage & Family Review, 59*(1), 6–35. https://doi.org/10.1080/01494929.2022.2125480

CHAPTER 3

Bioecological Theory

Basic premise	
Key figures	
Epistemology	
Assumptions	
Concepts	
Level of analysis	
Relevant studies	

Theory Overview

As per the goal of the text outlined in the preface, this chapter is a general overview of bioecological theory. This overview focuses on explaining the theory in a way that gives professionals who work with families (like family scientists) a solid understanding of it. Following the presentation of the theory, some considerations for practice are provided to assist with the application of the theory across a variety of contexts.

Contemporary bioecological theory is most associated with Urie Bronfenbrenner (1979). The theory examines how human-environment interactions shape a person's physical, social, and cultural development.

The bioecological theory has several assumptions guiding it (Bronfenbrenner, 1979; Smith & Hamon, 2022). Five assumptions of the theory are as follows:

- The bioecological hypothesis holds that human development is impacted by various interacting systems throughout life.
- It assumes that the environment influences growth and is constituted of various, interrelated systems.
- The theory also assumes that the environment is dynamic and that people adapt to these changes.
- It also assumes that people can shape their surrounding environment and their own development.
- The theory assumes that development takes time and that people change and adapt to their environment.

Bioecological theory is based on a variety of epistemologies (Bronfenbrenner, 1979; Bueno et al., 2015) or ways of knowing. These include constructivism (the bioecological paradigm says that interactions with the environment create knowledge), systems thinking (bioecological theory focuses on understanding the individual-environment system), contextualism (bioecological theory takes context into account), interactionism (bioecological theory focuses on how people and the environment interact), and ecological.

Basic Premise

This theory is used to explain how human individual and group (e.g., family) development happens through the interaction of person-environment interactions at multiple levels of context, with proximal processes as the driving force of development that shapes the lives of families and their members (Tudge and colleagues, 2009, 2016; Lerner and colleagues, 2008, 2009).

The contemporary usage of the theory is the PPCT (person, process, context, and time), which is a framework for comprehending how people interact with their environment and develop over time. It was created by Urie Bronfenbrenner and is based on the notion that people are intertwined with several layers of environmental systems, each of which affects how they grow (Bronfenbrenner & Morris, 2006, pp. 793–828).

The PPCT model stresses how important it is to understand how the different parts of the PPCT interact with each other and affect a person's development.

Key Figures

Both social and "hard" scientists contributed to bioecological theory. Darwin's (1859) theory of evolution by natural selection was a major addition to ecological theory. Evelyn Hutchinson's (1957) work on niche and community structure advanced ecological theory. MacArthur and Wilson (1967) write that island biogeography and species-area relationships advanced ecological theory. Ernst Haeckel's (1866) ecological theory holds that organisms are interrelated and the environment impacts species development. He hypothesized a "web of life" where changes in one species affect others. He also believed that environmental changes can cause new species to evolve. Swallow Richards's ecological theory of behavior (Barker, 1968) says that the environment determines behavior. She believed that the environment affects individual behavior and that people adapt to it. She suggested that environmental cues like food or animals can influence behavior. She suggested that environmental rewards and punishments can affect behavior. Ecological theory, as posited by Robert E. Park and Ernest W. Burgess (1925) and Giddens (2020), proposes that cities grow in rings from the city center outward. According to the hypothesis, the innermost ring is the densest and most impoverished. Outward from the city center, population density falls while economic and social status rises. Urie Bronfenbrenner (1979) began his work on ecological development in the 1970s, which morphed into the PPCT model in the mid-2000s. Since then, Jonathan Tudge and colleagues (2013 and 2022) have written extensively about the PPCT model.

Key Concepts

The following are concepts put forward by Brofenbrenner over the course of his work on the theory. See Tudge (2009) for an extended discussion of the concepts.

PPCT

The four components of the bioecological model emphasize the importance of understanding the interactions between the individual, the environment, and the context in which the individual lives.

Proximal Processes

Proximal processes are the everyday interactions between the developing individual or group and their immediate environment and are the driving force of growth.

Person Characteristics

Characteristics are the traits of the individual that have an effect on how the person interacts with their surroundings (knowledge, beliefs, attitudes, values, age, gender, and emotions).

Context

The microsystem, mesosystem, exosystem, and macrosystem are the four primary parts of the environment.

- **Microsystem.** The immediate environment in which an individual lives, including family, peers, school, and neighborhood.
- **Mesosystem.** The connections between different microsystems, such as the relationship between an individual's family and school.
- **Exosystem.** The indirect environment in which an individual lives, such as the workplace of a parent or the policies of a school district.
- **Macrosystem.** The larger cultural context in which an individual lives, such as the economic, political, and social environment.
- **Chronosystem.** The temporal dimension of the environment, including changes in the environment over time.

Time

Time in the PPCT model is the same as the chronosystem.

Synergy

The idea that two or more things working together can generate an effect bigger than the sum of their separate effects is used to emphasize that all aspects of the PPCT model work together to drive human development.

Considerations for Application

The following is a listing and brief description of some conceptual and empirical papers that use bioecological theory in different ways.

Conceptual Theorizing About the Bioecological Model

Harding et al. (2015) used bioecological This paradigm illuminates how maternal education changes proximal and distal influences on children's academic performance and how these processes interact and reinforce each other across time and environment.

Rose (2018) used the PPCT model to explain the intergenerational effects that Canada's residential school program had on the indigenous families who were forced to endure it.

Lewton and Nievar (2012) used the bioecological model to posit that family engagement in volunteering activities is a way to strengthen the connections between, and functioning of, the family unit.

Saxena and Adamsons (2013) used a bioecological lens to organize the literature on sibling relationships and developmental outcomes in the context of families who have a member with a developmental disability.

Cox et al. (2011) used the bioecological model to organize the multidisciplinary literature on Latino adolescent substance use in the United States.

Cao et al. (2016) used a number of theories, including bioecological theory, to discuss the unique experience of identity transformation that occurs among same-sex couples during the transition to parenthood.

Tudge et al. (2016) reviewed the literature for examples of papers that used the PPCT model to frame their theory and examine the extent to which those studies tested the theory as presented by the authors of the theory. While the theory has much popularity, Tudge et al. found that most papers misuse the theory, and that only 2 of 20 (Benson & Buehler, 2012; Farrant & Zubrick, 2012) papers actually tested and/or evaluated the theory in an appropriate manner.

Empirical Tests and Reviews of the Bioecological Model

Orthner et al. (2009) used the National Longitudinal Study of Youth (1997) to examine how family factors influence educational achievement and high school graduation. They found that living with two biological parents and family stability correlated with graduation, while parental marital quality and the parent-adolescent relationship were more predictive of postsecondary education access.

Li et al. (2014) looked at how different levels of conflict affect how a family works by using the bioecological model. They tested the theory on a sample of middle- and high school-aged youth in mainland China. In short, they were able to show that family functioning was affected by family (family socioeconomic status or SES), dyadic (parent-adolescent conflict), and individual (filial piety values) level factors. Further, the authors used the following instruments in their study:

- Chinese Family Assessment Instrument (Shek, 2002) used to assess family functioning.

- Family Social Environment Scale: used to capture parent-adolescent conflict with questions derived from both the typology of family social environment measure (Moos & Moos, 1976) and the four-factor index of social status (Hollingshead, 1975).
- Filial Piety Scale: developed based on the work of Yeh and Bedford (2003) and Yang et al. (1989).

Perry-Jenkins and Macdermid Wadsworth (2017) used an ecological perspective to review the work-family research published over a 40-year period (i.e., 1960s–2000) and how the research changed in response to changing contexts (e.g., theory development, cultural and historical changes).

Zhag and Han (2020) used bioecological theory to examine how varying spheres of influence are connected to multiple dimensions of poverty. Specifically, their longitudinal study used data from the Early Childhood Longitudinal Study (kindergarten class of 1998–1999) and latent class analysis to examine how varying dimensions of poverty are linked to behavioral responses in children over time.

McWey et al. (2008) used ecological theory, across three policy periods spanning the years of 1980–1997, to examine how Virgina (USA) courts terminated parental rights and the factors that appeared to be linked with increased termination of rights (e.g., parental mental health, parental IQs) and those factors that did not appear to impact parental termination of rights (e.g., parental substance abuse, presence of child special needs).

Fagan and Press (2008) used ecological theory to examine how family structure and dynamics impact heterosexual couples' rating of work-family balance. Relying on data from the Philadelphia Survey of Child Care and Work, this study found that the extent to which fathers brought more stress home from work and the extent to which fathers' jobs were flexible and allowed for them to be involved in childcare was linked to mothers' perception of successful work-family balance.

Conclusion

Bioecological theory explains the complexity of family life and how it is impacted by many environments. It stresses perceiving the family as a system, with each member impacting and being impacted by the others. Practitioners can better grasp each family's needs and adjust solutions by considering the many environments in which they reside. Bioecological family work fosters positive development and a supportive atmosphere for families.

Discussion Questions

1. How does the bioecological model explain the influence of culture on development?
2. What are the implications of the bioecological model and the PPCT model for research and practice?
3. What are the four systems of the bioecological model and how do they interact?
4. Explain the role of proximal processes in how a family develops.

References

Barker, R. G. (1968). *Ecological psychology: Concepts and methods for studying the environment of human behavior.* Stanford University Press.

Benson, M. J., & Buehler, C. (2012). Family process and peer deviance influences on adolescent aggression: Longitudinal effects across early and middle adolescence. *Child Development, 83*(4), 1213–1228. https://doi.org/10.1111/j.1467-8624.2012.01763.x

Bronfenbrenner, U. (1979). *The ecology of human development: Experiments by nature and design.* Harvard University Press.

Bronfenbrenner, U., & Morris, P. (2006). *The bioecoloigical model of human development.* Wiley.

Bueno, R. K., Vieira, M. L., Crepaldi, M. A., & Schneider, D. R. (2015). Epistemological considerations of bioecological perspective on human development about father involvement. *Psicologia em Revista, 21*(3), 599–620.

Cao, H., Roger Mills-Koonce, W., Wood, C., & Fine, M.A. (2016). Identity transformation during the transition to parenthood among same-sex couples: An ecological, stress-strategy-adaptation perspective. Journal of Family Theory & Review, 8, 30–59. https://doi-org.proxy.lib.miamioh.edu/10.1111/jftr.12124

Cox, R. B., Jr., Burr, B., Blow, A. J., & Parra Cardona, J. R. (2011). Latino adolescent substance use in the united states: Using the bioecodevelopmental model as an organizing framework for research and practice. *Journal of Family Theory & Review, 3,* 96–123. https://doi-org.proxy.lib.miamioh.edu/10.1111/j.1756-2589.2011.00086.x

Darwin, C. (1859). *On the origin of species by means of natural selection, or the preservation of favoured races in the struggle for life.* John Murray.

Fagan, J., & Press, J. (2008). Father influences on employed mothers' work–family balance. *Journal of Family Issues, 29*(9), 1136–1160. https://doi-org.proxy.lib.miamioh.edu/10.1177/0192513X07311954

Farrant, B. M., & Zubrick, S. R. (2012). Early vocabulary development: The importance of joint attention and parent-child book reading. *First Language, 32*(3), 343–364. https://doi.org/10.1177/0142723711422626

Giddens, A. (2020). Ernest W. Burgess. In *Encyclopedia Britannica*. https://www.britannica.com/biography/Ernest-W-Burgess

Haeckel, E. (1866). *Generelle morphologie der organismen.* G. Reimer.

Harding, J. F., Morris, P. A., & Hughes, D. (2015). The relationship between maternal education and children's academic outcomes: A theoretical framework. *Journal of Marriage and Family, 77*(1), 60–76. https://doi-org.proxy.lib.miamioh.edu/10.1111/jomf.12156

Hollingshead, A. B. (1975). *Four factor index of social status* [Unpublished working paper]. Department of Sociology at Yale University. https://sociology.yale.edu/sites/default/files/files/yjs_fall_2011.pdf#page=21

Hutchinson, G. E. (1957). *The ecological theater and the evolutionary play.* Yale University Press.

Lerner, R. M., & Lerner, J. V. (2008). *Theoretical models of human development* (6th ed.). Wiley.

Lerner, R. M., & Lerner, J. V. (Eds.). (2009). *Handbook of child psychology: Theoretical models of human development* (Vol. 1, 6th ed.). Wiley.

Lewton, A. R., & Nievar, M. A. (2012). Strengthening families through volunteerism: Integrating family volunteerism and family life education. *Marriage & Family Review, 48*(7), 689–710, https://doi.org/10.1080/01494929.2012.700909

Li, X., Zou, H., Liu, Y., & Zhou, Q. (2014). The relationships of family socioeconomic status, parent–adolescent conflict, and filial piety to adolescents' family functioning in mainland China. *Journal of Child and Family Studies, 23*, 29–38. http://dx.doi.org/10.1007/s10826-012-9683-0

MacArthur, R. H., & Wilson, E. O. (1967). *The theory of island biogeography.* Princeton University Press.

McWey, L. M., Henderson, T. L., & Burroughs Alexander, J. (2008). Parental rights and the foster care system: A glimpse of decision making in Virginia. *Journal of Family Issues, 29*(8), 1031–1050. https://doi-org.proxy.lib.miamioh.edu/10.1177/0192513X08316542

Moos, R. H., & Moos, B. S. (1976). A typology of family social environments. *Family Process, 15*(4), 357–371. https://doi.org/10.1111/j.1545-5300.1976.00357.x

Navarro, J. L., Stephens, C., Rodrigues, B. C., Walker, I. A., Cook, O., O'Toole, L., Hayes, N., & Tudge, J. R. (2022). Bored of the rings: Methodological and analytic approaches to operationalizing Bronfenbrenner's PPCT model in research practice. *Journal of Family Theory & Review, 14*(2), 233–253.

Orthner, D. K., Jones-Sanpei, H., Hair, E. C., Moore, K. A., Day, R. D., & Kaye, K. (2009). Marital and parental relationship quality and educational outcomes for youth. *Marriage & Family Review, 45*, 2–3, 249–269. https://doi.org/10.1080/01494920902733617

Park, R. E., & Burgess, E. W. (1925). *The city.* University of Chicago Press.

Rosa, E. M., & Tudge, J. (2013). Urie Bronfenbrenner's theory of human development: Its evolution from ecology to bioecology. *Journal of Family Theory & Review, 5*(4), 243–258.

Rose, H. A. (2018), "I didn't get to say good-bye ... didn't get to pet my dogs or nothing": Bioecological theory and the Indian residential school experience in Canada. *Journal of Family Theory & Review, 10*, 348–366. https://doi.org/10.1111/jftr.12261

Saxena, M., & Adamsons, K. (2013), Siblings of individuals with disabilities: Reframing the literature through a bioecological lens. *Journal of Family Theory and Review, 5*, 300–316. https://doi.org/10.1111/JFTR.12021

Shek, D. T. (2002). Assessment of family functioning in Chinese adolescents: The Chinese family assessment instrument. *International Perspectives on Child and Adolescent Mental Health, 2*, 297–316. https://doi.org/10.1016/S1874-5911(02)80013-6

Smith, S., & Hamon, R. (2022). *Exploring family theories.* Oxford University Press.

Tudge, J. (2009). The bioecological model of human development. In R. M. Lerner & W. Damon (Eds.), *Handbook of child psychology: Theoretical models of human development* (Vol. 1, 6th ed., pp. 793–828). Wiley.

Tudge, J. R., Mokrova, I., Hatfield, B. E., & Karnik, R. B. (2009). Uses and misuses of Bronfenbrenner's bioecological theory of human development. *Journal of Family Theory & Review, 1*(4), 198–210.

Tudge, J. R., Payir, A., Merçon-Vargas, E., Cao, H., Liang, Y., Li, J., & O'Brien, L. (2016). Still misused after all these years? A reevaluation of the uses of Bronfenbrenner's bioecological theory of human development. *Journal of Family Theory & Review, 8*(4), 427–445.

Yang, K. S., Yeh, K. H., & Huang, L. L. (1989). A social attitude analysis of Chinese filial piety: Conceptualization and assessment. *Bulletin of the Institute of Ethnology, 56*, 171–227 (in Chinese).

Yeh, K. H., & Bedford, O. (2003). A test of the dual filial piety model. *Asian Journal of Social Psychology, 6*(3), 215–228. https://doi.org/10.1046/j.1467-839X.2003.00122.x

Zhang, L., & Han, W.-J. (2020). Uncovering multidimensional poverty experiences in shaping children's socioemotional trajectories during the first 6 years of schooling. *Family Process, 59*, 1837–1855. https://doi.org/10.1111/famp.12530

CHAPTER 4

Conflict Theory

Basic premise	
Key figures	
Epistemology	
Assumptions	
Concepts	
Level of analysis	
Relevant studies	

Theory Overview

As per the goal of the text outlined in the preface, this is a general overview of conflict theory, as it relates to families. This overview focuses on explaining the theory in a way that helps professionals who work with families, like family scientists, do their jobs better. After the theory is explained, some considerations for practice are given that can be used in a variety of settings.

Conflict theory has its roots in sociology and addresses conflict within and between humans. Some of the earlier writers focused on issues such as the nature of mankind (e.g., the extent to which they carry out their lives to satisfy their self-interests), competition in marketplaces, and how that can result in inequalities. The sociological roots of the theory focused more on macrolevel issues, but the theory has also been applied to micro contexts (e.g., individuals and families), such as to show that the condition of conflict is always present when observing human interactions. The theory is based on a positivist epistemology, which means that its proponents often use data to show that conflict is always present when people interact. Though reasons for the presence of conflict, and how it is managed or resolved vary, conflict is nevertheless present in human interactions. This leads to the assumption of the theory, which is that conflict is inevitable in the human experience. Put another way, conflict is an inevitable part of life. Here, we are discussing families and the conflict that exists with them in light of having to manage the scarce resources available to them.

Conflict theory can be applied at multiple levels (macro, micro, mezzo), but this chapter will focus more on how the theory can be applied when engaging families. For instance, family conflict can be examined internally (family members may experience conflict with each other) or externally (one family has conflict with another family). For an extended discussion on the history and trajectory of conflict theory, as it relates to families, see Allen and Henderson (2023, Ch. 3), Farrington and Chertok (1993, pp. 357–381), Smith and Hamon (2022, Ch. 6), and White et al. (2015, Ch. 7).

The study of how knowledge is created and applied in the setting of social conflict is known as the epistemology of conflict theory. Its foundation is the notion that knowledge is socially created and used to uphold privilege and power in society (Giroux, 2001). It is a critical method for comprehending the creation, application, and contestation of knowledge in social contexts. It is focused on how information is employed to uphold and legitimize current power structures.

Basic Premise

The basic premise of this theory is to explain conflict within and between families. A major explanation for why conflict exists within families is due to the allocation and distribution of resources (e.g., time, energy, knowledge, housing, money, food, skills, education[1]). Resources are the material things humans use to satisfy their needs and desires (Sowell, 2014). But an important quality of resources is that they are scarce, finite, or limited. Therefore, humans must consider the trade-offs they must make to receive all or some of the things they want and desire. The competition for scarce resources creates conflict among social groups of humans because each is self-interested in securing the needed resources to satisfy their needs. Several concepts of conflict theory have been advanced to better understand the nature of conflict in families.

Key Figures

There are several works you should consider reading to better understand how conflict works within and between individuals and groups, to include families. I have listed some here, though this is only a brief listing. I encourage you to seek out additional resources if this is a topic of study that is of interest to you. I have grouped together some conflict theorists based on how the given scholar contributed to the theory.

- Conflict within individuals
  - ▷ Machiavelli (2014)
  - ▷ Hobbes (Hobbes & Missner, 2016)
  - ▷ Sowell (2002)
- Resource-based conflict in groups
  - ▷ Marx (Marx & Engels, 1848)
  - ▷ Sen (2007)
  - ▷ Coser (1998)
- Conflict within families
  - ▷ Sprey (1969, 1971, 1972, 1979, 1999)
  - ▷ Baxter (2021)
  - ▷ Thibaut and Kelley (1959)

Key Concepts

Several FST are presented here in hopes of aiding scholars and practitioners in applying the theory in context.

---

1 This is a brief listing of family resources that can be found in families. For an extended discussion on family resources, see Moore and Asay's (2018) foundational text on the topic.

Conflict. A disagreement between two or more parties.[2]

Conflict Management. Actively addressing the disagreement between parties without a resolution.

Conflict Resolution. An ending of a dispute or disagreement whereby the opposing parties come to a consensus about the disagreement.

Resources. Things people desire that have scarce quantities and alternative uses.

Capital. The intangible or tangible abilities and currency that can be used to obtain desired resources.

Competition. The inevitable struggle between parties is due to each desire to obtain more resources that are available to the many entities who desire it.

Considerations for Application

Conflict theory can be applied to the family unit to understand how power dynamics and competition for resources can lead to conflict within the family. For example, when one family member has more power than the others, they may use this power to control resources and decision-making, leading to tension and conflict within the family (Britannica, n.d.).

Family theory can be applied to the family unit to understand how different family structures and dynamics can affect the family's functioning. For example, a family with a strong hierarchical structure may be more likely to experience conflict due to unequal power dynamics, while a family with a more egalitarian structure may be more likely to experience cooperation and collaboration (Simple Psychology, n.d.).

Macrolevel

Golash-Boza (2016) attributes conflict between groups (e.g., families) based on racial differences and negative actions toward others who don't share racial features (e.g., racism). This paper argues that race and racism have a structure in society that advantages some while disadvantaging others.

Pettigrew's (1998) classic paper articulates a theory of intergroup contact. Specifically, the theory focuses on the roots of human social interactions,

---

2   It is possible for a sole member of a family to have an internal dispute (even toward another member) without other members of the family being aware of the other family member's internal feelings. This can certainly also cause family conflict.

more specifically the development and maintenance of intergroup conflict within social interactions. Adding to this, Sidanius and Pratto (1999) discuss the specifics of social interactions and how hierarchies and opportunities develop in social settings.

Microlevel

At the microlevel, Sue et al. (2007) discuss how personal interactions between individuals, who are different on given characteristics (e.g., race and ethnicity), can lead to intentional or unintentional actions that are subtly harmful to others. Examples may take the form of jokes, sly comments, and culturally taboo actions.

Tucker et al.'s (2003) paper examined conflict resolution styles within family units, looking specifically at gender differences in how adolescents resolve conflict within family units. Findings revealed that both boys and girls were better at conflict resolution strategies with their parents relative to siblings, and better conflict resolution strategies were linked to better adjustment. In another study with adolescents and parents, Van Doorn et al. (2008) found that poor conflict resolution between adolescents and their parents (i.e., both mothers and fathers) was linked to increased delinquency for adolescents.

Conclusion

Family dynamics can be better understood using conflict theory. It aids in our comprehension of how authority and resources are allocated within a family and how this might cause conflict. We can better comprehend how family members interact with one another and how this can cause conflict. The conflict theory has also been used to describe how social and economic influences, for example, might have an impact on family relations. Policies and interventions that can aid families in better managing conflict and enhancing their relationships can be informed by conflict theory. Understanding how families work and how to handle conflict within them are two things that conflict theory can help with.

Discussion Questions

1. How does conflict theory explain the power dynamics within families?
2. How does conflict theory view the role of gender in family dynamics?
3. How can conflict theory help us to understand the dynamics of family relationships?

4. How can families use conflict theory to resolve conflicts in a constructive way?
5. How can families use conflict theory to create a more equitable and harmonious home environment?
6. What are some of the potential benefits of using conflict theory to understand family dynamics?

References

Allen, K. R., & Henderson, A. C. (2017). *Family theories: Foundations and applications.* Wiley Blackwell.

Baxter, L. A., Scharp, K. M., & Thomas, L. J. (2021). Relational dialectics theory. *Journal of Family Theory & Review, 13*(1), 7–20. https://doi.org/10.1111/jftr.12405

Britannica (n.d.). Conflict theory. In *Britannica.com.* https://www.britannica.com/topic/conflict-theory

Coser, L. A. (1998). *The functions of social conflict* (Vol. 9). Routledge.

Farrington, K., & Chertok, E. (1993). *Sourcebook of family theories and methods.* Springer.

Giroux, H. A. (2001). *Theory and resistance in education: A pedagogy for the opposition.* Bergin & Garvey.

Golash-Boza, T. (2016). A critical and comprehensive sociological theory of race and racism. *Sociology of Race and Ethnicity, 2*(2), 129–141. https://doi.org/10.1177/2332649216632242

Hobbes, T., & Missner, M. (2016). *Thomas Hobbes: Leviathan (Longman library of primary sources in philosophy).* Routledge.

Machiavelli, N. (2014). *The prince and other writings.* Simon and Schuster.

Marx, K., & Engels, F. (1848). The communist manifesto. *Selected Works by Karl Marx and Frederick Engels.* International Publishers.

Moore, T. J., & Asay, S. M. (2017). *Family resource management.* SAGE Publications.

Pettigrew, T. F. (1998). Intergroup contact theory. *Annual Review of Psychology, 49,* 65–85. https://doi.org/10.1146/annurev.psych.49.1.65

Sen, A. (2007). *Identity and violence: The illusion of destiny.* Penguin Books India.

Sidanius, J., & Pratto, F. (1999). *Social dominance: An intergroup theory of social hierarchy and oppression.* Cambridge University Press.

Smith, S., & Hamon, R. (2022). *Exploring family theories.* Oxford University Press.

Sowell, T. (2002). *A conflict of visions: Ideological origins of political struggles.* Basic Books.

Sowell, T. (2014). *Basic economics.* Basic Books.

Sprey, J. (1969). The family as a system in conflict. *Journal of Marriage and the Family, 31,* 699–706.

Sprey, J. (1971). On the management of conflict in families. *Journal of Marriage and the Family, 34*(4), 722–731.

Sprey, J. (1972). Family power structure: A critical comment. *Journal of Marriage and Family, 34*(2), 235–238.

Sprey, J. (1979). Conflict theory and the study of marriage and the family. In W. R. Burr, R. Hill, & F. I. Nye (Eds.), *Contemporary theories about the family* (Vol. 2., pp. 130–159). Free Press.

Sprey, J. (1999). Family dynamics. In M. Sussman, S. K. Steinmetz, & G. W. Peterson (Eds.), *Handbook of marriage and the family* (pp. 667–685). Springer.

Sue, D. W., Capodilupo, C. M., Torino, G. C., Bucceri, J. M., Holder, A. M. B., Nadal, K. L., & Esquilin, M. (2007). Racial microaggressions in everyday life: Implications for clinical practice. *American Psychologist, 62*(4), 271–286. https://doi.org/10.1037/0003-066X.62.4.271

Thibaut, J. W., & Kelley, H. H. (1959). *The social psychology of groups.* Wiley.

Tucker, C., McHale, S., & Crouter, A. (2003). Conflict resolution: Links with adolescents' family relationships and individual well-being. *Journal of Family Issues, 24*(6), 715–736. https://doi.org/10.1177/0192513X03251181

Van Doorn, M., Branje, S., & Meeus, W. (2008). Conflict resolution in parent-adolescent relationships and adolescent delinquency. *The Journal of Early Adolescence, 28*(4), 503–527. https://doi.org/10.1177/0272431608317608

White, J. M., Martin, T. F., & Adamsons, K. (2015). *Family theories: An introduction.* SAGE Publications.

CHAPTER 5

Social Exchange Theory

Basic premise	
Key figures	
Epistemology	
Assumptions	
Concepts	
Level of analysis	
Relevant studies	

Theory Overview

Per the goal of the text outlined in the preface, this is the general overview of social exchange theory as it relates to families. This overview focuses on explaining the theory in a way that helps professionals who work with families, like family scientists, do their jobs better.

After the theory is explained, some considerations for practice are given that can be used in a variety of settings.

White et al. (2015) say that social exchange theory is based on epistemological or intellectual traditions like utilitarianism and rational choice thinking. It looks at what makes people decide what to do in social situations. More specifically, this theory has been used in studying families to understand factors that undergird human decision-making. This theory has typically been applied at the microlevel of analysis, typically focusing on dyadic relationships.

Basic Premise

Social exchange theory is a theoretical perspective in sociology and psychology that explains how individuals make decisions in relationships based on the costs and benefits of interactions. Social exchange theory is based on the idea that people form relationships with other people to get the most out of the relationships and pay the least amount of costs for and in relationships. Rewards can include things like love, companionship, and emotional support, while costs can include things like time, effort, and emotional distress. The theory says that people are smart (or rational) and weigh the costs and benefits of relationships before making decisions. Also, people are more likely to start and keep relationships when they think the benefits are greater than the costs. Social exchange theory is based on the idea that relationships are formed and maintained through the process of exchange, where each party gives and receives something of value. Several assumptions guide social exchange theory:

- Human beings are rational and make decisions based on cost-benefit analysis (Thibaut & Kelley, 1959).
- Human beings are motivated to maximize rewards and minimize costs in their relationships (Foa & Foa, 1974).
- Human beings compare their outcomes with those of others to evaluate their own relationships (Homans, 1961).
- Human beings are motivated to maintain relationships that are perceived to be equitable (Walster et al., 1978).

Key Figures

Homans (1958, 1961) is widely considered the founder of modern social exchange theory. His work focused on the exchange of rewards and punishments between individuals in a social setting. He argued that people use rewards and punishments as motivation and that they use these to assess the worth of a relationship. Blau's (1964) work focused on the exchange of resources between individuals in a social setting. Emerson (1976) argued that people are motivated to exchange resources to maximize their own benefit and that the value of a relationship is determined by the resources exchanged. Additional key figures include the following:

- Cropanzano and Mitchell: *Exchange Theory: An Interdisciplinary Review* (2005)
- John Thibaut and Harold Kelley: *The Social Psychology of Groups* (1959), *Interpersonal Relations: A Theory of Interdependence* (1978)
- Ron Sabatelli: *Social Exchange Theories* (2022)

Key Concepts

Reciprocity
The concept that people exchange resources such as favors, goods, and services in exchange for something of equal or greater value.

Resources
Things desired that have limited quantity (scarcity) and alternative uses.

Equity
The notion that people should be provided with a fair and equitable exchange of resources.

Social Norms
The behavioral expectations that are accepted by a specific group or society.

Power
The ability to influence other people's behavior.

Trust
The concept that another person will act in a reliable and consistent manner.

Comparison Level
A standard representing what people feel they should receive in the way of rewards and costs from a particular relationship.

Comparison Level for Alternative

Refers to the lowest level of relational rewards a person is willing to accept in comparison to being alone, given the available rewards from alternative relationships.

Principle of the Least Interested

The principle of the least interested suggests that the person who is least invested in a relationship has the most power to influence the dynamics of the relationship (Felmlee, 1994).

Considerations for Application

Family scientists have for a long time used social exchange theory to explain family dynamics (Sabatelli, 2022, pp. 259–277; Sabatelli & Shehan, 1993). In the context of family interactions, this means that family members may act in ways they think will lead to positive outcomes or rewards, such as love, approval, or support from other family members, while minimizing costs or negative outcomes, such as conflict, rejection, or emotional distress. There are a variety of ways that social exchange theory can explain family interactions.

Exchange of Resources

The social exchange theory says that people interact with each other to trade resources they think are valuable. In the family context, this can involve the exchange of material resources, such as money or possessions, or nonmaterial resources, such as emotional support or caregiving (Daspit et al., 2016; Edwards, 1969; Safilios-Rothschild, 1976; Thomas et al., 2017).

Costs and Benefits of Family Roles

Social exchange theory suggests that individuals consider the costs and benefits of their actions before making decisions. In the family context, this can involve considering the costs and benefits of different family roles, such as being a parent, spouse, or child (Grossbard-Schechtman, 2019; Hin, 2017; Parsons et al., 2015; Sassler & Lichter, 2020). For example, being a parent can take a lot of time and energy, but it can also offer benefits or rewards in terms of emotional satisfaction and social status.

Reciprocity in Family Relationships

Social exchange theory says that people tend to do good things for those they care about. In the family context, this means that family members may engage in behaviors that they believe will result in positive responses from other family members (Schwarz et al., 2005; Van Dijk, 2020, pp. 173–196; Walker et al., 1992). For example, if a parent praises and rewards a child for doing well in school, the child may want to keep doing well so that they can get more praise and rewards in the future.

Impact of Perceived Fairness on Family Interactions

According to social exchange theory, people are motivated to maximize their rewards while incurring the fewest costs, and their sense of fairness plays a role in this process. DeMaris and Mahoney (2017), Maier and Priest (2016), and Qian and Sayer (2016) have found that how people feel about marriage is linked to a number of family-related outcomes, such as satisfaction with family relationships, trust in family relationships, conflict in family relationships, and even the survival of relationships.

Conclusion

Social exchange theory has been used to explain family relationships for many years. This theory suggests that family members interact with one another in an effort to maximize their rewards and minimize their costs. Through this process, family members are able to maintain a balance of power and resources. This balance is achieved through the exchange of resources, such as love, support, and respect.

In conclusion, social exchange theory provides a valuable framework for understanding family relationships. This theory can help us to better understand how family members interact with one another and how they strive to maintain a balance of power and resources (Kelley & Thibaut, 1978). By understanding the dynamics of family relationships, there is an opportunity to better support families and help them to create healthy, positive relationships.

Discussion Questions

1. How does social exchange theory help explain the dynamics of family relationships?
2. How do the concepts of "costs" and "rewards" and "equity" shape family relationships?
3. How do family members balance their own needs with those of other family members?

4. How does social exchange theory help explain the development of family roles and responsibilities?
5. How does social exchange theory help explain the dynamics of family conflict, loyalty, and commitment?

References

Blau, P. M. (1964). *Exchange and power in social life.* Transaction Publishers.

Cropanzano, R., & Mitchell, M. S. (2005). Social exchange theory: An interdisciplinary review. *Journal of Management, 31*(6), 874–900.

Daspit, J. J., Holt, D. T., Chrisman, J. J., & Long, R. G. (2016). Examining family firm succession from a social exchange perspective: A multiphase, multistakeholder review. *Family Business Review, 29*(1), 44–64.

DeMaris, A., & Mahoney, A. (2017). Equity dynamics in the perceived fairness of infant care. *Journal of Marriage and Family, 79*(1), 261–276.

Edwards, J. N. (1969). Familial behavior as social exchange. *Journal of Marriage and the Family, 31*(3), 518–526.

Emerson, R. M. (1976). Social exchange theory. *Annual Reviews, 2,* 335–362. https://doi.org/10.1146/annurev.so.02.080176.002003

Felmlee, D. H. (1994). Who's on top? Power in romantic relationships. *Sex Roles, 31*(5–6), 275–295. https://link.springer.com/article/10.1007/BF01544589

Foa, U. G., & Foa, E. B. (1974). *Societal structures of the mind.* Charles C. Thomas.

Grossbard-Schectman, S., & Grossbard-Shechtman, S. (2019). *On the economics of marriage.* Routledge.

Hin, O. K. (2017). Child marriages in Malaysia: Reality, resistance, and recourse. *Penang Institute Issues, 2.*

Homans, G. C. (1958). Social behavior as exchange. *American Journal of Sociology, 63*(6), 597–606. http://www.jstor.org/stable/2772990

Homans, G. (1961). *Social behavior: Its elementary forms.* Harcourt, Brace & World.

Kelley, H. H., & Thibaut, J. W. (1978). *Interpersonal relations: A theory of interdependence.* Wiley.

Maier, C. A., & Priest, J. B. (2016). Perceived fairness, marital conflict, and depression: A dyadic data analysis. *The American Journal of Family Therapy, 44*(2), 95–109.

Parsons, J., Edmeades, J., Kes, A., Petroni, S., Sexton, M., & Wodon, Q. (2015). Economic impacts of child marriage: A review of the literature. *The Review of Faith & International Affairs, 13*(3), 12–22.

Qian, Y., & Sayer, L. C. (2016). Division of labor, gender ideology, and marital satisfaction in East Asia. *Journal of Marriage and Family, 78*(2), 383–400.

Sabatelli, R. M. (2022). *Sourcebook of family theories and methodologies: A dynamic approach.* Springer International Publishing.

Sabatelli, R. M., & Shehan, C. L. (1993). Exchange and resource theories. In P. Boss, W. Doherty, R. LaRossa, W. Schumm, & S. Steinmetz (Eds.), *Sourcebook of family theories and methods: A contextual approach* (pp. 385–417). Springer.

Safilios-Rothschild, C. (1976). A macro-and micro-examination of family power and love: An exchange model. *Journal of Marriage and Family, 38*(2), 355–362.

Sassler, S., & Lichter, D. T. (2020). Cohabitation and marriage: Complexity and diversity in union-formation patterns. *Journal of Marriage and Family, 82*(1), 35–61.

Schwarz, B., Trommsdorff, G., Albert, I., & Mayer, B. (2005). Adult parent–child relationships: Relationship quality, support, and reciprocity. *Applied Psychology, 54*(3), 396–417.

Thibaut, J. W., & Kelley, H. H. (1959). *The social psychology of groups.* Routledge.

Thomas, P. A., Liu, H., & Umberson, D. (2017). Family relationships and well-being. *Innovation in Aging, 1*(3), igx025.

Van Dijk, R. (2020). *The transnational family.* Routledge.

Walker, A. J., Pratt, C. C., & Oppy, N. C. (1992). Perceived reciprocity in family caregiving. *Family Relations, 41*(1), 82–85.

Walster, E., Walster, G. W., & Berscheid, E. (1978). *Equity: Theory and research.* Allyn & Bacon.

White, J. M., Martin, T. F., & Adamsons, K. (2015). *Family theories: An introduction.* SAGE Publications.

CHAPTER 6

Structural Functionalism Theory

Basic premise	
Key figures	
Epistemology	
Assumptions	
Concepts	
Level of analysis	
Relevant studies	

Theory Overview

As per the goal of the text outlined in the preface, this is a general overview of structural functionalism theory. This overview focuses on explaining the theory in a way that helps professionals who work with families, like family scientists, do their jobs better. Following the presentation of the theory, some considerations for practice are provided to assist with application of the theory across a variety of contexts.

The theory takes on a positivist worldview, with an assumption that the family has an important function in society. The theory has been applied at multiple levels, though the early writings focused on society and how its derivative parts function to fit into that society.

Structural functionalism theory is framed by a series of assumptions about society, its components, the functions of those components, and how their structures and interrelatedness contribute to the stability of society (Durkheim, 1893; Macionis & Plummer, 2005; Parsons, 1953).

Holism of social systems. Social structures and institutions are interdependent, and changes in one part of the system can have ripple effects throughout the rest of the system.

Interrelated social systems contribute to social order. Structural functionalism argues that societies are complex systems made up of various interdependent parts and that each part has a specific function that contributes to the overall stability and well-being of the society.

Shared values and norms create stable societies. To maintain social order, the social structures (e.g., families, schools, institutions, organizations, laws) must be based on shared values and norms, which guide individual behavior and provide a sense of order and predictability for individuals and groups (e.g., families). Moreover, through a process of socialization, individuals are taught the values and norms of their society and learn to conform to them. For example, parents in family systems socialize children to the norms and values of society or maybe join social institutions (e.g., religions) that assist with the development and maintenance of socializing shared beliefs and values.

Social stability or change occurs over time. When social structures have shared beliefs and values that are followed by many citizens, there is a social equilibrium that creates order and stability. Conversely, where any disruptions or changes to the system occur, there will eventually be compensated for through various mechanisms of adaptation (i.e., social change).[1]

Basic Premise

Structural functionalism is a sociological theory about the structure and functioning of organized units. During the theory's inception, the primary unit of focus was societies and their individuals. The theory was developed between the mid-19th and early 20th centuries and focused on factors such as the changing nature of societies, where goods were produced via agricultural means before becoming produced via more industrialized means. Such changes had social ramifications for individuals, communities, and families. In the 20th century, one of the theory's more prominent theorists (Talcott Parsons) used structural functionalism to make assertions about families.

Understanding and applying this theory requires understanding that organizing units typically have a structure as well as a function. Hence, structural functionalism. Importantly, this can be used for people, families, communities, societies, etc., on many different levels.[2]

Key Figures

Emile Durkheim's contribution to theory (Bellah, 2017, pp. 3–26; Durkheim, 1893, 1895/1982, 1912/2001) was about the importance of social order and solidarity. Social organizations and institutions (e.g., religion) play an important role in providing a mechanism for social solidarity through shared values and beliefs. This can then be used to strengthen the social order and cohesion that are needed for society to work well.

Herbert Spencer (1860, 1876) added to the theory by looking at it from the points of view of social evolution and functional interrelatedness. He contended that society is made up of a number of interconnected social institutions (e.g., government, family, and religion) that work together to maintain social order. Each of the social institutions plays a unique role in the development and maintenance of a stable society. The social evolution perspective linked together the notion that societies evolve over time and that those that have

---

1   This assumption here, whether realized or not, is one explanation for why political and social (e.g., religious) systems in the United States have such strong feelings about family structures and family life. Depending on their view of society and its functioning, there are arguments for too much or too little change.

2   Much more can be learned about structural functionalism by visiting ScienceDirect's website on structural functionalism at https://www.sciencedirect.com/topics/social-sciences/structural-functionalism.

the "fittest" social institutions are better able to create the "fittest" societies that survive and thrive.

Talcott Parsons's (1955) work added significantly to the theory as a whole, much of which continue to have relevance in contemporary thinking about families and family life. As with the other theorists we've talked about, Parsons's work was mostly about social structures and how they affect how society works. In terms of families, Parsons (1955) argued that nuclear families are the most important functional unit for social stability, reproduction, and the socialization of certain beliefs and values. Parsons's work from 1956 and 1968/2013 also talks about gender roles in families. He says that all families have to meet the needs of their members through two functional roles: instrumental (financial support and family status) and expressive (emotional and physical care). Parsons suggested that men take on the instrumental roles and women take on the expressive roles.

Robert Merton's (1938) contribution to the theory was based on how social structures affect how people act. He argued that social structures can create strains and subsequent deviant behavior.

Key Concepts

- **Deviance:** deviance is a disconnect between the cultural goals of a society and means available for individuals to achieve cultural goals.
- **Strain:** process whereby the cultural goals that all society members are pressured to achieve or live up to produce strain.
- **Roles:** structural functionalism has two primary [conceptual] roles within a family.
  - ▷ *Expressive:* roles that attend to the emotional needs of the family and its members.
  - ▷ *Instrumental:* roles that tend to the tangible needs of the family.[3]
- **Solidarity:** the shared values, beliefs, and norms that bind individuals together in a society and create a sense of unity and collective identity. It is the glue that holds society together and allows it to function. Solidarity is essential for a society to be able to function, as it provides a sense of belonging and purpose to individuals.
- **Interrelated systems:** concept of structural functionalism theory that views society as a complex system of interconnected systems (cultural, personality, social) parts that work together to promote stability and balance. It focuses on the way in which social structures and institutions,

---

3   When these concepts were first introduced in the mid-20th century, instrumental roles were assigned to men and expressive roles to women, which is likely why the theory has struggled to remain relevant in contemporary times. See Pittman's 1993 paper for more on this topic.

such as family, education, and religion, contribute to the maintenance of a society's stability. The theory argues that social structures are functional and that they serve a purpose in maintaining the social order. It also suggests that social change is a slow and gradual process, and that any changes should be made carefully and with consideration of the effects it may have on the entire system.

Considerations for Application

The theory of structural functionalism has been applied to families at multiple levels of context (macro, mezzo, and micro).

Societal or Macrolevel Application

Zvinkliene (1996) used structural functionalism theory to analyze the state of families in Lithuania. This macrolevel look at how structural-functional theory focuses on how theory was used to guide the study of families and explain how society was changing. Cseh-Szombathy and Somlai (1996) used the same approach to study Hungarian families. Other examples are available in that same volume (22) and issue (1–2) of *Marriage & Family Review* (*MFR*).

Mezzo- or Community- and Family-Level Application

Scanzoni (2001) used the theory of structural functionalism to study how households, which are part of a community, have structural features that help shape the community, which in turn affects the way families and communities work together.

Micro- or Family-Level of Application

Voris and Steinkopf (2019) used structural functionalism to investigate the familial experience of the wives of combat veterans. In particular, the problems they face because of the roles they play and the expectations that come with those roles.

Historically, structural functionalism theory explains how families have changed over time. By looking at family roles and relationships, family scholars can learn how families have changed over time to fit in with society. Structural functionalism theory has been used to study the functioning of family systems across cultures. Family scholars can better understand global family systems by comparing family functions across contexts. By figuring out what social roles families play, structural functionalism theory can help policymakers make programs to help families. Family scholars can learn about families in different social, economic, and cultural contexts by comparing their functions.

Conclusion

Over the decades, structural functionalism theory has fallen out of favor in family science for a variety of reasons. Even though many people may not agree with the positivist view (that social processes can be seen objectively; Alharahsheh & Pius, 2020) or the way family roles have been gendered (Bales & Parsons, 2014), the theory still applies to how families are set up and what they do in society (Pittman, 1993).

Theories change over time, and others offer more nuanced and complex explanations of social phenomena than structural functionalism. Additionally, structural functionalism theory has been criticized for being too simplistic and failing to account for power differentials and social conflicts. It assumes a stable, harmonious society, which is not always true. Also, the assumptions and predictions of structural functionalism theory may not always match up with the complexity of real-life family life.

The theory is still useful today because, among other things, it shows how the functions of social institutions depend on each other.[4] One example could be how the theory helps explain the bidirectional relationship between organizing units. In the context of studying families, this would mean how families are important to society and society is important to families (which can be graphically represented as Society ↔ Family). This bidirectional relationship can be observed in multiple countries or states around the globe. The point is that there is a bidirectional relationship between families and state-level entities, whether we are discussing one-child policies in China (Potts, 2006), payments to families to increase fertility rates in Sweden (McDonald, 2000), or general state-based social safety nets to promote family well-being (Gassman-Pines & Hill, 2013). They depend on each other in a symbiotic relationship. However, it is certainly true that the theory derives from sociological theory, so much of it has been used to study macrolevel issues (see *Marriage & Family Review*, 1996, Vol. 22, Iss. 1–2, for several examples). However, as shown earlier, the theory can also be used at other levels of context (mezzo and micro). The key for practitioners to be mindful of prior to applying this theory is to know their goals for engaging families and applying this theory. If the goal is related to

---

4   Though the examples are many, a few contemporary examples of structural functioning thinking across multiple levels of contexts is warranted. The new University of Colorado's football coach's approach to recruiting quarterbacks, specifically how family structure produces certain attributes in player abilities (Morik, 2023). Also, though trends in family life are shifting, many Americans still have strong preferences for certain types of families (Cox, 2022). Finally, at the macrolevel, decision-making in families has significant impact on various aspects of society (e.g., economy), or even its existence (Ahn, 2023; Ripley et al., 2023). All of these examples reflect structural functionalism thinking in contemporary times.

the structure or function of families or some other level of an organizational unit, this theory has much potential for application.

Discussion Questions

1. What time period was this theory born? What was society like? How did families function when the theory emerged relative to contemporary times?
2. Provide an example of how families depend on society for well-being.
3. Provide an example of how the state government depends on families for the health of society.
4. Reflect on the roles that members of your family had. What rationale supported that a given role was best for a given family member?

References

Ahn, A. (2023, March 19). *South Korea has the world's lowest fertility rate, a struggle with lessons for us all.* NPR. https://www.npr.org/2023/03/19/1163341684/south-korea-fertility-rate

Alharahsheh, H. H., & Pius, A. (2020). A review of key paradigms: Positivism VS interpretivism. Global Academic *Journal of Humanities and Social Sciences, 2*(3), 39-43. DOI: 10.36348/gajhss.2020.v02i03.001

Bales, R. F., & Parsons, T. (2014). *Family: socialization and interaction process.* Routledge.

Bellah, R. N. (2017). *Emile Durkheim.* Routledge.

Cox, D. A. (2022, February 2022). *Emerging trends and enduring patterns in American family life.* Survey center on American life. American Enterprise Institute. https://www.americansurveycenter.org/research/emerging-trends-and-enduring-patterns-in-american-family-life/

Cseh-Szombathy, L., & Somlai, P. (1996). Family theory and research in Hungary. *Marriage & Family Review, 22*(3–4), 181–201. https://doi-org.proxy.lib.miamioh.edu/10.1300/J002v22n03_01

Durkheim, E. (1893). *The division of labor in society.* Free Press.

Durkheim, E. (1982). *The rules of sociological method.* Palgrave. (Original work published 1895)

Durkheim, E. (2001). *The elementary forms of religious life.* Oxford University Press. (Original work published 1912)

Gassman-Pines, A., & Hill, Z. (2013). How social safety net programs affect family economic well-being, family functioning, and children's development. *Child Development Perspectives, 7*(3), 172–181. https://doi.org/10.1111/cdep.12037

Macionis, J. J., & Plummer, K. (2005). *Sociology: A global introduction*. Pearson Education.

McDonald, P. (2000). *The "toolbox" of public policies to impact on fertility—a global view*. ANU Research Publications. https://openresearch-repository.anu.edu.au/handle/1885/41446

Merton, R. K. (1938). Social structure and anomie. *American Sociological Review, 3*(5), 672–682.

Merton, R. K. (1996). *On social structure and science*. University of Chicago Press.

Morik, R. (2023, February 28). *ESPN analyst takes offense to Deion Sanders' recruiting tactics: "This s--- ain't funny."* Fox Sports. https://www.foxnews.com/sports/espn-analyst-takes-offense-deion-sanders-recruiting-tactics-this-s-t-aint-funny

Parsons, T. (1953). *A revised analytical approach to the theory of social stratification*. Harvard University Press.

Parsons, T. (1955). Family structure and the socialization of the child. In T. Parsons & R. Bales (Eds.), *Family, socialization and interaction process* (pp. 3–43). Routledge.

Parsons, T. (1956). Family structure and the social system. In R. N. Anshen (Ed.), *The family: Its function and destiny* (pp. 27–40). Harper.

Parsons, T. (2013). *The social system*. Routledge. (Original work published 1968)

Pittman, J. F. (1993). Functionalism may be down, but it surely is not out. Another point of view for family therapists and policy analysts. In P. G. Boss, W. J. Doherty, R. Larossa, W. R. Schumm, & S. K. Steinmetz' (Eds.), *Sourcebook of family theories and methods. A contextual approach* (pp. 218–224). Springer Science & Business Media.

Potts, M. (2006). China's one child policy. *BMJ, 333*(7564), 361–362. https://doi.org/10.1136/bmj.38938.412593.80

Ripley, W., Ogura, J., & Sugiura, N. (2023, March 19). *This community's quarter century without a newborn shows the scale of Japan's population crisis*. CNN. https://www.cnn.com/2023/03/17/asia/japan-population-crisis-countryside-cities-intl-hnk-dst/index.html

Scanzoni, J. (2001). A personal and intellectual journey. *Marriage & Family Review, 31*(1–2), 139–160.

Spencer, H. (1860). The social organism. In H. Spencer (Ed.), *Essays* (Vol. 1, pp. 265–307). Williams and Norgate.

Spencer, H. (1876). *The principles of sociology*. Williams and Norgate.

Voris, S. E., & Steinkopf, J. (2019). Suffering in the shadows: Interviews with wives of combat veterans suffering from post-traumatic stress disorder and/or traumatic brain injury. *Marriage & Family Review, 55*(6), 493–511. https://doi-org.proxy.lib.miamioh.edu/10.1080/01494929.2018.1519494

Zvinkliene, A. (1996). The state of family studies in Lithuania. *Marriage & Family Review, 22*(3–4), 203–232. https://doi.org/10.1300/J002v22n03_02

CHAPTER 7

Relational Developmental Systems Theory

Basic premise	
Key figures	
Epistemology	
Assumptions	
Concepts	
Level of analysis	
Relevant studies	

Theory Overview

As per the goal of the text outlined in the preface, this is a general overview of relational developmental systems (RDS) theory. This overview focuses on explaining the theory in a way that helps professionals who work with families, like family scientists, do their jobs better. After the theory is explained, some things to think about in practice are given to help the theory be used in a variety of situations.

RDS theory is a theory of human development that, when considering a text about human families, can help explain the relationship between human development and the family in which people are reared. RDS also argues that human development occurs through interactions at multiple levels of context. This interaction occurs both within the individual and between the individual and their environment. This perspective considers the multiple aspects of the person and how interactions that shape development, such as having particular features in certain environments, can produce developmental opportunities or constraints. Let's consider this example: Being LGBTQ+ and a person of faith in the U.S. state of Alabama brings certain constraints compared to having similar features and characteristics in the U.S. state of California. This example considers the contexts of the individual (sexuality), community (religion), and macro (geographic state), all of which combine to shape human development. Other things, like the beliefs and habits of the person's family, would also affect the person's opportunities or limitations.

RDS theory is a broad theoretical framework that comes from many different fields, such as sociology, human genetics, and developmental science (Lerner & Benson, 2013). The RDS theory does stress how important empirical research is, but it also acknowledges how important subjective experiences, context, and social interactions are to how people grow and change. RDS theory focuses on how different developmental systems, such as a person's biology and psychology, family systems, peer groups, and larger societal contexts, are all connected. The theory also emphasizes the importance of understanding and promoting positive developmental outcomes rather than simply focusing on the prevention of negative outcomes. So, RDS is agile in research and practice and can support several epistemological approaches.

RDS are known to emphasize several key features (Lerner & Callina, 2013, pp. 373–374). The key features include the following:

- RDS models put a lot of emphasis on the study and integration of different levels of organization, as a way to understand how people change over the course of their lives.

- RDS models emphasize mutually influential relations between individuals and contexts, represented as individual $\leftrightarrow$ context relations.
- RDS models emphasize the rules and processes that govern or regulate exchanges between individuals and their contexts.
- RDS models argue that when developmental regulations involve mutually beneficial individual $\leftrightarrow$ context relations, then these developmental regulations are *adaptive*.
- RDS models emphasize the presence of (relative) plasticity in human development, which ushers in the potential for systematic change in individual $\leftrightarrow$ context relations. This potential comes from the connections between the person and the different levels of their changing environment.
- RDS models emphasize that all development is embedded within history and the ubiquitous presence of dynamic and systematic change across multiple levels of context.

Basic Premise

RDS is a way of thinking about how people grow and change over time. It claims that interaction between people and their surroundings shapes development, which is a dynamic process. It is based on the idea that individuals are embedded in multiple contexts, such as family, peers, and culture, and that these contexts interact to shape development. RDS says that it's important to understand how people and their environments affect each other and how this affects development over time. RDS also says that people are active participants in their own development and that they can make choices and change their surroundings (Lerner & Barton, 2020; Lerner et al., 2015).

Key Figures

Richard Lerner, Willis Overton, Marc H. Bornstein, and Peter Benson have all studied or used RDS, especially when it comes to family relationships. Bornstein (2005) argued that the development of children is best understood in terms of the interplay between the child, the family, and the wider social environment. Additionally, the family environment is one of the most important things that affects how a child grows up, and the quality of the family environment is shaped by how the parents interact with each other, the wider social context, and how the child acts. Overton's (2006) and Lerner's (2002) work helped to shape RDS, which is a way to study human development that looks at it from many different angles. Overton and Lerner's work focuses on how important relationships are to development. They also stress the role of context and how development is always changing. One important idea is that people can change and adapt to their environments and relationships in order to help their growth. Lastly, but not least, another name to be familiar with is Peter Benson. Benson (2006, 2008) used RDS thinking to develop his work on youth development and thriving. His work led to the development of assets and developmental relationship programs, which are used in many places to help children and young people grow up in a healthy and positive way. His work consistently championed the role of parents in helping their children thrive.

Because of the current literature on positive youth development, I talk about these specific groups of scholars who have written about this theory, and I do so in a certain order. People who work with families understand that most families desire to provide the best opportunity to help their children thrive. Many of the positive youth development models (e.g., developmental assets, the 5 C's of positive youth development (PYD), youth participatory action research (YPAR)) can all be categorized as RDS-based models.

Key Concepts

RDS theory is a set of ideas that emphasizes how important it is for a person's development that they interact with their social environment. RDS proposes that development occurs through a dynamic, bidirectional process of interactions between individuals and their environments and that these interactions occur across multiple levels of analysis, from the micro to the macro. Some key concepts of RDS include (Lerner, 2006; Overton, 2015):

Multidirectionality

Development happens in many different ways, and gains and losses happen at the same time in different areas of functioning.

Plasticity

People have the ability to change and adapt throughout their lives in response to their environments.

Historical Embeddedness

The social, cultural, and historical context in which development takes place has an impact on a person's course of development.

Multiple Levels of Analysis

Among other things, interactions between the individual, family, community, and culture shape development.

Individual-Context Relations

The way a person interacts with their social environment affects how they grow and change. Both the individual and their environment shape each other.

PYD theory is a framework that focuses on the good parts of adolescent development (without ignoring the negative) and encourages young people to build on their strengths instead of just focusing on their problems (Catalano et al., 2004).

Some of the most important ideas in developmental assets and relationships frameworks (Benson et al., 2004; Search Institute, 2021), the 5 C's of PYD (Lerner et al., 2005), and YPAR literature (Checkoway & Richards-Schuster, 2003) are as follows:

Developmental Assets

Developmental assets are the good experiences, relationships, and chances that help a person grow and become successful as an adult. There are 40 developmental assets that support PYD, 20 of which are internal and 20 of which are external. Some of these assets are good family communication, community service, and creative activities.

Developmental Relationships

The PYD theory emphasizes the importance of positive relationships between youth and adults, as well as among peers. These connections give young people support, direction, and chances to improve their social skills.

5 C's of PYD

The 5 C's represent five key qualities that young people need to become healthy, productive, and successful adults. These C's include competence, confidence, connection, character, and caring.

Youth Voice and Engagement

The PYD theory encourages young people to have a voice in their own development and to be actively engaged in the decisions that affect their lives. This approach promotes autonomy, self-esteem, and a sense of ownership over their own development.

Considerations for Application

RDS theory can be applied to families, especially youth development, in a number of ways. The applications here align with the aforementioned presentation of concepts.

Developmental Assets Literature

The literature on developmental assets identifies several ways in which parents can help their children thrive (Search Institute, 2021, 2023).

Build Strong Relationships with Children

Parents who have close and supportive relationships with their children are more likely to help them develop positive values and behaviors.

Provide Opportunities for Children to Develop Skills and Interests

Parents who encourage their kids to do things outside of school or to pursue hobbies can help them build confidence, competence, and a sense of purpose.

Set Clear Boundaries and Expectations

The American Academy of Pediatrics says it's important to set clear rules and expectations for children's behavior and give them consequences when they don't meet those expectations.

Foster a Sense of Community and Belonging

The Search Institute notes that children who feel connected to their families, schools, and communities are more likely to develop positive attitudes and behaviors.

Model Positive Behaviors and Attitudes

According to the American Psychological Association, parents who model positive behaviors and attitudes, such as empathy, kindness, and self-control, can help their children develop those same qualities.

Developmental Relationships Literature

The literature on developmental relationships highlights several ways in which parents can help their children thrive by fostering strong, positive relationships. Here are some key findings, along with relevant sources and references (Search Institute, 2021, 2023):

Prioritize Quality Time with Children

According to the Search Institute, kids can learn to trust and feel like they belong if their parents spend quality time with them and have meaningful conversations and activities with them.

Listen Actively and Show Empathy

Active listening and empathy in building strong relationships with children help them feel heard and understood.

Encourage Independence and Responsibility

Parents who encourage their children to take on responsibilities and make decisions for themselves can help them develop a sense of competence and self-efficacy.

Be a Positive Role Model

Parents who act and think in positive ways, like showing respect, being responsible, and being honest, can help their kids do the same.

Support Children's Interests and Passions

Parents who support their children's interests and passions, even if they differ from their own, can help them develop a sense of purpose and identity.

5 C's of PYD

The 5 C's of PYD model emphasizes five key competencies that can help young people thrive. Here are some ways in which parents can support these competencies (Lerner, 2008; Lerner et al., 2005; Lerner et al., 2015).

Competence

Competence refers to skills and abilities in areas such as academic performance, social skills, and decision-making. Parents can help their kids become more competent by giving them chances to learn and grow, such as by signing them up for extracurricular activities or encouraging them to take up hobbies.

Confidence

Confidence involves developing a sense of self-efficacy and belief in one's abilities. Parents can help their kids feel more confident by praising and encouraging their achievement efforts and by helping them set and reach goals.

Connection

Connection involves developing strong, positive relationships with others. Parents can help their kids connect by encouraging open communication, giving them emotional support, and helping them make friends and find mentors.

Character

Character involves developing values and beliefs that promote positive behaviors and attitudes. Parents can help their children develop good character by setting a good example, teaching them to be responsible and respectful, and giving them chances to take part in service and civic activities.

Caring

Caring involves developing empathy and concern for others. Parents can encourage caring by showing empathy, getting their kids to think about how other people feel, and giving them chances to do acts of kindness and service.

Big Three Factor Model

The *Big Three Factors* of the applied PYD framework identify three primary factors that can help youth thrive: relationships, opportunities, and skills (Lerner, 2008). Here are some ways in which parents can support these factors.

Relationships

The relationship factor involves building strong, positive, and sustained connections with adults and peers. Parents can help relationships by being present and involved in their children's lives, giving emotional support, and helping their children build positive relationships with mentors and peers.

Opportunities

The opportunity factor is about giving young people chances to learn, grow, and help their communities. Parents can help their kids get opportunities by encouraging them to try new things and find new interests, by doing community service projects with them, and by helping them reach their educational and career goals.

Skills

The skill factor is about getting better at things like communication, leadership, and solving problems. Parents can help their children develop skills by giving them chances to use and improve them, such as by getting them involved in group projects, encouraging them to take on leadership roles, and giving them constructive feedback and direction.

Conclusion

RDS theory is a big-picture way to look at how people grow and change and how they interact with their environments. Applying the principles of PYD to RDS highlights how important it is to give young people positive relationships and supportive environments to help them grow up healthy.

When applied to families, RDS and PYD offer valuable insights into the ways in which parents and caregivers can support their children's growth and well-being. Families can set the stage for their children's healthy development and future success by putting an emphasis on positive relationships, open communication, and supportive environments.

Discussion Questions

1. How can families apply RDS principles to support PYD in their children?
2. What are some challenges that families may face in applying PYD principles to their parenting approach?
3. How can community organizations and resources support families in fostering PYD within the context of RDS?
4. How might cultural or societal factors impact the ways in which families apply RDS and PYD principles to their parenting?

References

Benson, P. L. (2006). *All kids are our kids: What communities must do to raise caring and responsible children and adolescents.* Jossey-Bass.

Benson, P. L. (2008). *Sparks: How parents can ignite the hidden strengths of teenagers.* John Wiley & Sons.

Benson, P. L., Scales, P. C., Hawkins, J. D., Oesterle, S., & Hill, K. G. (2004). *Successful young adult development. A report submitted to: The Bill & Melinda Gates Foundation.* http://www.search-institute.org/system/files/GatesFdnReport-EmergingAdulthood2004.pdf

Bornstein, M. H. (2005). Parenting: A dynamic systems framework. In M. H. Bornstein (Ed.), *Handbook of parenting: Being and becoming a parent* (Vol. 3, 2nd ed., pp. 1–17). Lawrence Erlbaum Associates.

Catalano, R. F., Berglund, M. L., Ryan, J. A., Lonczak, H. S., & Hawkins, J. D. (2004). Positive youth development in the United States: Research findings on evaluations of positive youth development programs. *The Annals of the American Academy of Political and Social Science, 591*(1), 98–124. https://doi.org/10.1177/0002716203260102

Checkoway, B., & Richards-Schuster, K. (2003). Youth participation in community evaluation research. *American Journal of Evaluation, 24*(1), 21–33. https://doi.org/10.1177/109821400302400103

Lerner, R. M., & Barton, C. E. (2000). Adolescents as agents in the promotion of their positive development: The role of youth actions in effective programs. *Control of human behavior, mental processes, and consciousness: Essays in honor of the 60th birthday of August Flammer* (pp. 457–475). Psychology Press.

Lerner, R. M. (2002). *Concepts and theories of human development* (3rd ed.). Lawrence Erlbaum Associates.

Lerner, R. M. (2006). Developmental science, developmental systems, and contemporary theories of human development. In R. M. Lerner (Ed.), *Handbook of child psychology: Theoretical models of human development* (Vol. 1, pp. 1–17). John Wiley & Sons.

Lerner, R. M. (2008). *The good teen: Rescuing adolescence from the myths of the storm and stress years*. Harmony.

Lerner, R. M., & Benson, J. B. (2013). *Embodiment and epigenesis: Theoretical and methodological issues in understanding the role of biology within the relational developmental system: Part A, philosophical, theoretical, and biological dimensions*. Academic Press.

Lerner, R. M., & Callina, K. S. (2013). Relational developmental systems theories and the ecological validity of experimental designs. *Human Development, 56*(6), 372–380. https://doi.org/10.1159/000357179

Lerner, R. M., Johnson, S. K., & Buckingham, M. H. (2015). Relational developmental systems-based theories and the study of children and families: Lerner and Spanier (1978) revisited. *Journal of Family Theory & Review, 7*(2), 83–104. https://doi.org/10.1111/jftr.12067

Lerner, R. M., Lerner, J. V., Almerigi, J., Theokas, C., Phelps, E., Gestsdottir, S., Naudeau, S., Jelicic, H., Alberts, A., Ma, L., Smith, L., Bobek, D., Richman-Raphael, D., Simpson, I., Christiansen, E. D., & von Eye, A. (2005). Positive youth development, participation in community youth development programs, and community contributions of fifth-grade adolescents: Findings from the first wave of the 4-H Study of Positive Youth Development. *Journal of Early Adolescence, 25*(1), 17–71. https://doi.org/10.1177/0272431604272461

Overton, W. F. (2006). Dynamic systems of development: Action and interaction. In W. Damon & R. M. Lerner (Eds.), *Handbook of child psychology: Theoretical models of human development* (Vol. 1, 6th ed., pp. 567–634). John Wiley & Sons.

Overton, W. F. (2015). Relational developmental systems. In R. M. Lerner (Ed.), *Handbook of child psychology and developmental science* (Vol. 1, pp. 9–62). John Wiley & Sons.

Search Institute (2021). *Developmental assets framework*. https://www.search-institute.org/developmental-assets/developmental-assets-framework/

Search Institute (2023). *Developmental relationships framework*. https://info.searchinstitute.org/developmental-relationships-help-young-people-thrive

CHAPTER 8

Feminist Theory

Basic premise	
Key figures	
Epistemology	
Assumptions	
Concepts	
Level of analysis	
Relevant studies	

Theory Overview

As per the goal of the text outlined in the preface, this is a general overview of feminist theory. This overview focuses on explaining the theory in a way that helps professionals who work with families, like family scientists, do their jobs better. After the theory is explained, some things to think about in practice are given to help the theory be used in a variety of situations.

Basic Premise

Feminism is about the equal treatment and valuing of the sexes within society. The theory can be used in micro (how couples divide chores among family members) or macro policies that try to equalize the sexes. Feminist theory is a multidisciplinary approach that tries to figure out why there are differences between men and women, why women are oppressed, and how patriarchal structures are made and kept in society. At its core, feminist theory is about challenging and changing the social, economic, and political systems that keep inequality and oppression between men and women in place.

Overall, feminist theory tries to show how gender shapes our social world and gives ways to challenge and change the structures that keep inequality and oppression between men and women going. Feminist theory is based on several assumptions about the nature of gender and power in society. While there is some variation in these assumptions across different strands of feminist thought, the following are some commonly cited characteristics:

Gender is Socially Constructed

Feminist theory assumes that gender is not a natural or biological category but rather a socially constructed identity that is created and reinforced through social norms, cultural values, and institutional practices (Butler, 1990; West & Zimmerman, 1987).

Patriarchy is a Pervasive System of Power

Feminist theory posits that patriarchy, or the social and political dominance of men over women, is a pervasive system of power that shapes all aspects of social life, including institutions, cultural practices, and individual behavior (Beauvoir, 1949; hooks, 1984; Smith, 1989).

Women's Experiences are Marginalized

Feminist theory recognizes that women's experiences are often left out of or ignored by dominant social narratives and that their points of view are important for understanding how gender inequality and oppression work (Collins, 1990; Lorde, 1984).

Intersectionality Matters

Feminist theory recognizes the ways in which gender intersects with other social categories, such as race, class, sexuality, and disability, to create unique forms of oppression and privilege (Anzaldúa, 1987; Crenshaw, 1991; Collins, 2000).

Action is Necessary for Change

Feminist theory assumes that change is possible and that action is necessary to challenge and transform the patriarchal systems that perpetuate gender inequality and oppression (hooks, 2000; Mohanty, 2003).

Key Figures

Different "waves" of feminist activism and scholarship have been grouped into different parts of feminist theory. These waves show how feminist ideas and the political and social environments have changed, which has changed the goals and strategies of feminist movements. There is more than one way to categorize the waves of feminist theory, but the following is a common framework:

First Wave Feminism: The first wave of feminism emerged in the late 19th and early 20th centuries and focused primarily on gaining suffrage and other legal and political rights for women. Susan B. Anthony was a key figure in the suffrage movement during the first wave of feminism.

Second Wave Feminism: The second wave of feminism emerged in the 1960s and 1970s and was characterized by a focus on women's social and cultural rights, as well as their experiences of oppression in the family and workplace. *The Feminine Mystique* by Betty Friedan is thought to have played a significant role in the second wave of feminism.

Third Wave Feminism: The third wave of feminism emerged in the 1990s. It focused on intersectionality and diversity, recognizing that multiple social identities, like race, class, sexuality, and disability, affect how women are oppressed. The movement became more inclusive of more diverse voices and perspectives (e.g., Clenora Weems, Kimberlé Crenshaw).

Fourth Wave Feminism: The fourth wave of feminism is often seen as a continuation and evolution of the third wave, characterized by a focus on online activism, the #MeToo movement (e.g., Tarana Burke), and a renewed emphasis on challenging gender-based violence and harassment.

Key Concepts

Feminist theory is a large and varied field that looks at things from many different points of view. However, there are some key concepts that are central to much feminist thought. The following is a nonexclusive list of some concepts from the theory:

Gender
Feminist theory says that gender is a social and cultural construct that affects how people live and what opportunities they have (Butler, 1990).

Patriarchy
Patriarchy refers to a system of social organization in which men hold primary power and authority and women are systematically excluded from positions of power and authority (hooks, 1984).

Intersectionality
Intersectionality is the way that different social categories, like gender, race, class, and sexuality, interact and overlap to shape experiences of privilege and oppression (Crenshaw, 1991).

Power
Foucault (1990) says that power is a key concept for understanding social relationships and how they shape the experiences of both individuals and groups.

Agency
Feminist theory acknowledges the agency and capacity of individuals and groups to resist and challenge systems of power and oppression (hooks, 2000).

Social Justice
Feminist theory is often concerned with issues of social justice, such as giving power and resources to groups that have been left out and making social structures that are fairer (Mohanty, 2003).

Praxis
The call to action that moves feminist theory to feminist practice and action (Stanley, 2013).

Considerations for Application

In a variety of ways, feminist theory has been applied to the study of families, shedding light on issues of power, inequality, and gender roles within family structures. There are several ways that feminist theory has been and can be used to engage and/or understand families, in both general ways and in various specific areas of family life.

General

There are several examples of how feminist theory relates to general aspects of family life.

Division of Labor

Feminist theory has been used to criticize the traditional roles of men and women in families, especially how men and women divide up the work. Scholars have said that traditional gender roles can make differences between men and women worse within families and keep larger patterns of inequality between men and women going (Hochschild, 1989).

Domestic Violence

Domestic violence and how it affects families have been brought to more people's attention thanks to feminist theory. Scholars have used feminist frameworks to analyze the social and cultural contexts that contribute to domestic violence, as well as the ways in which survivors of domestic violence resist and challenge these patterns of abuse (Dobash & Dobash, 1979).

Reproductive Labor

Feminist theorists have also looked at the role of women in reproductive work, such as having children, raising them, and taking care of the sick or elderly. Scholars have said that this kind of work is often undervalued and not paid, and that it helps keep gender inequality in society as a whole (Folbre, 1994).

LGBTQ Families

Feminist theory has also been used to understand the experiences of LGBTQ families, including the ways in which gender and sexual orientation intersect to shape family dynamics and relationships. Scholars have used intersectional frameworks to learn about how LGBTQ families are different and to challenge heteronormative ideas about how families should be set up (Goldberg & Allen, 2013).

Marriage and Parenting

There are several examples of how feminist theory relates to specific components of family life. Feminist theory has been applied to the study of marriage and parenting, illuminating the ways in which gender, power, and inequality intersect within these contexts.

Power Dynamics in Marriage

Feminist theorists have criticized traditional gender roles and how they can make marriages more unequal in terms of power. For example, some people have said that the idea that women should do more housework when they get married can make them less important in the economy and society (Connell, 2013).

Division of Labor in Parenting

Feminist scholars have also studied the ways in which parenting is gendered and how that affects the division of labor in parenting. They argue that women's mothering roles have been traditionally valued more than men's fathering roles, and this has led to women doing more unpaid care work, which can have an impact on their work-life balance (Yavorsky et al., 2015).

Fatherhood and Masculinities

Feminist theory can also be used to study fatherhood and masculinity. For example, Pleck (2010) looked at how dominant forms of masculinity might affect how men parent and care for their children.

Reproductive Justice

Feminist scholars (Luna & Luker, 2013: Ross, 2006) have used the idea of "reproductive justice" to look at how marriage, parenting, and reproductive decisions fit into larger patterns of inequality and social justice.

Conclusion

Applying feminist theory to the study of families has been a valuable way to understand the ways in which gender, power, and inequality intersect within family structures. Scholars have used feminist frameworks to criticize traditional gender roles, bring attention to domestic violence, look at how women's work in reproductive work is undervalued, and study how LGBTQ families are different. Feminist theory has also been used to study marriage and parenting, shedding light on how power works in relationships, how men and women divide up the work of parenting, and how dominant forms of masculinity affect fatherhood.

Overall, feminist theory has highlighted the ways in which families are not neutral but rather are shaped by broader patterns of gender inequality and power dynamics. By examining the ways in which these dynamics play out within families, scholars and practitioners can work toward promoting more equitable and just family lives for all members of the family.

Discussion Questions

1. How do traditional gender roles and expectations impact family dynamics? What are some examples of ways in which these roles can be challenged or subverted?
2. In what ways do the patriarchy and the gendered division of labor contribute to gender inequality within families? How might feminist theory inform efforts to promote more equitable divisions of labor?
3. How might feminist theory be applied to issues of domestic violence and abuse within families? What are some ways in which feminist frameworks can help to address these issues?
4. How do issues of reproductive justice intersect with family structures? In what ways might feminist theory inform discussions around access to reproductive health care and family planning?
5. How might the experiences of LGBTQ families challenge traditional notions of family structures and gender roles? What are some ways in which feminist theory can inform our understanding of these experiences?
6. How can a feminist perspective help to promote more equitable and just family structures? What are some potential challenges to implementing such changes?
7. These are just a few potential discussion questions, but they can help to spark conversation and critical thinking around the application of feminist theory to families.

References

Anzaldúa, G. (1987). *Borderlands/la frontera: The new mestiza.* Aunt Lute Books.

Beauvoir, S. d. (1949). *The second sex.* Vintage Books.

Butler, J. (1990). *Gender trouble: Feminism and the subversion of identity.* Routledge.

Collins, P. H. (1990). *Black feminist thought: Knowledge, consciousness, and the politics of empowerment.* Routledge.

Collins, P.H. (2000). *Black feminist thought: Knowledge, consciousness, and the politics of empowerment* (2nd ed.). Routledge.

Connell, R. (2013). *Gender and power: Society, the person and sexual politics.* John Wiley & Sons.

Crenshaw, K. (1991). Mapping the margins: Intersectionality, identity politics, and violence against women of color. *Stanford Law Review, 43*(6), 1241–1299.

Dobash, R. E., & Dobash, R. (1979). *Violence against wives: A case against the patriarchy* (Vol. 15). Free Press.

Folbre, N. (1994). *Who pays for the kids?: Gender and the structures of constraint* (Vol. 4). Taylor & Francis.

Foucault, M. (1990). *The history of sexuality: An introduction* (Vol. 1). Vintage.

Goldberg, A. E., & Allen, K. R. (Eds.). (2013). *LGBT-parent families: Innovations in research and implications for practice.* Springer.

Hochschild, A. R. (1989). *The second shift: Working parents and the revolution at home.* Viking.

hooks, b. (1984). *Feminist theory: From margin to center.* South End Press.

hooks, b. (2000). *Feminism is for everybody: Passionate politics.* Pluto Press.

Lorde, A. (1984). *Sister outsider: Essays and speeches.* Crossing Press.

Luna, Z., & Luker, K. (2013). Reproductive justice. *Annual Review of Law and Social Science, 9,* 327–352.

Mohanty, C. T. (2003). *Feminism without borders: Decolonizing theory, practicing solidarity.* Duke University Press.

Pleck, J. H. (2010). Fatherhood and masculinity. *The Role of the Father in Child Development, 5,* 27–57.

Ross, L. (2006). Understanding reproductive justice: Transforming the pro-choice movement. *Off Our Backs, 36*(4), 14–19.

Smith, D. E. (1989). *The everyday world as problematic: A feminist sociology.* Northeastern University Press.

Stanley, L. (Ed.). (2013). *Feminist praxis (RLE feminist theory): Research, theory and epistemology in feminist sociology.* Routledge.

West, C., & Zimmerman, D. H. (1987). Doing gender. *Gender & Society, 1*(2), 125–151.

Yavorsky, J. E., Kamp Dush, C. M., & Schoppe-Sullivan, S. J. (2015). The production of inequality: The gender division of labor across the transition to parenthood. *Journal of Marriage and Family, 77*(3), 662–679. https://doi.org/10.1111/jomf.12189

CHAPTER 9

Family Life Course

Basic premise	
Key figures	
Epistemology	
Assumptions	
Concepts	
Level of analysis	
Relevant studies	

Theory Overview

As per the goal of the text outlined in the preface, this is a general overview of family life course theory. This overview focuses on explaining the theory in a way that helps professionals who work with families, like family scientists, do their jobs better. After the theory is explained, some considerations for practice are discussed to help the theory be used in a variety of situations.

For this text, it is important to make a distinction between life course theory (a theory of human development) and family life course theory (an adapted version of life course theory when applied to families). Life course theory and family life course theory are two related concepts that focus on understanding the ways in which individuals and families develop over time.

Life course theory stresses how important it is to understand the social, cultural, and historical factors that shape a person's development. It shows how transitions and turning points shape individual paths and how important it is to understand how individual choice and social structure work together (Elder et al., 2003).

Family life course theory builds on life course theory but emphasizes the importance of understanding family processes and relationships over time. It emphasizes the interdependence of family members, the importance of developmental tasks at different stages of the family life cycle, and the ways in which family members support and shape each other's development (Bengtson & Allen, 1993).

Simply put, life course theory is a broader view that focuses on how important it is to understand how people change over time, while family life course theory looks at how processes and relationships affect how families change.

Basic Premise

Family life course theory is a way to look at how individual and family development change and interact with each other over the course of a person's life. It seeks to understand how individual development is influenced by family context and how family development is influenced by individual characteristics and life events. McGoldrick et al. (2013) note that families are seen as dynamic systems that evolve over time, responding to both internal and external changes.

Notably, the course of a family's life is a continuous process that is affected by many things, such as individual traits, the structure of the family, and cultural and societal norms. Elder et al. (2003) note that the family's life course can be divided into several stages, including the early years of marriage, the birth and infancy of children, the growth and development of children, the launching of children into adulthood, and the later years of life. From an epistemological point of view, this theory is mostly qualitative, focusing on the subjective experiences and points of view of people and families as they go through different stages and changes in life and emphasizing the importance of understanding the unique context and experiences of each family to gain insight into their development over time (Elder, 1998; Elder et al., 2003).

Family life course theory is built on several assumptions that shape its perspective on family development (De Jong & Graefe, 2008; Elder, 1998; Gilligan et al., 2018; Macmillan & Copher, 2005). These assumptions include the following:

Families are Complex Systems

Family life course says that families are complex systems that change and adapt to new situations all the time. Some examples of contributing factors include individual characteristics, family structure, cultural and societal norms, and historical and environmental contexts.

Families are Diverse

Family life course theory recognizes that families come in many different shapes and sizes and that there is no single "right" way to define or measure family functioning or development. Instead, the theory stresses how important it is to understand each family's unique history and experiences to understand how they change over time.

Family Development is Shaped by Transitions

Family life course theory emphasizes the importance of transitions or changes in family structure or roles that occur over time. These changes can be good or bad, planned or unplanned, and they can have a major impact effect on how well a family works and grows.

Development is Influenced by Both Past and Current Experiences

Family life course theory recognizes that individuals and families are influenced by both their past experiences and their current circumstances. This means that past experiences can have long-lasting effects on individual and family development over time.

Power and Privilege Shape Family Dynamics

Family life course theory recognizes that power and privilege play a role in how families work and what they do. The theory recognizes that families are situated within larger societal contexts and that cultural and structural inequalities can have a significant impact on family development and functioning.

Key Figures

Glen H. Elder Jr. and Rand Conger contributed to the development of a family life course perspective, including their project *Families in Troubled Times* (2020), which continues to shape family scholarship in contemporary times.

Arland Thornton is another scholar who has helped make family life course theory what it is today. He is best known for his work on social change and family relationships. (1997, 1994).

Judith S. Wallerstein is another scholar who has contributed to the development of family life course theory, particularly as applied to the long-term effects of divorce on children, which looks at how divorce affects children's development and well-being over time (Wallerstein, 1991; Wallerstein & Lewis, 2004).

Key Concepts

Family life course theory encompasses a range of key concepts that help to explain how individuals and families develop over time (Bengtson & Allen, 1993; De Jong & Graefe, 2008; Elder, 1998; Gilligan et al., 2018; Greenfield & Marks, 2006; Macmillan & Copher, 2005).

The following ideas give you a framework for understanding how families change and grow over time. Family life course theory helps us understand the many things that affect how families work and grow by looking at how people and families deal with changes, make decisions, and interact with their social and cultural environments.

Life Course Perspective

This concept emphasizes the importance of understanding the developmental trajectories of individuals and families over time and the ways in which they are shaped by social, cultural, and historical contexts.

Trajectories

Trajectories are the paths individuals take through life, shaped by individual characteristics and social and environmental factors. They can be stable or unstable and can be influenced by both personal agency and external constraints. Life course theory distinguishes between individual and cohort trajectories, with individual trajectories being unique and cohort trajectories being shared experiences and patterns of change.

Overall, the concept of trajectories is a central component of life course theory, highlighting the importance of understanding the complex and dynamic processes that shape individual development and change over time.

Cumulative Disadvantage and Advantage

Cumulative disadvantage and advantage describe the accumulation of positive or negative experiences and opportunities over the course of an individual's life. Negative experiences, such as poverty, poor health, and discrimination, can limit opportunities and create further disadvantages. Positive experiences, such as high-quality education, good health, and access to resources, can create further advantages. Life course theory suggests that the accumulation of disadvantage or advantage can have significant impacts on individual development and outcomes.

Transitions

This concept refers to changes in family structure, roles, and relationships that occur over time. Transitions can be good or bad, planned or unplanned, and they can have a major influence on how a family works and grows.

Timing

This concept refers to the idea that the timing of life events and transitions can have a significant impact on individual and family development. For example, the timing of marriage and parenthood can influence the trajectory of family development over time.

Agency

This concept refers to the idea that individuals and families have the ability to make choices and exert control over their own lives, even in the face of challenging circumstances.[1]

Social Context

This term refers to the idea that economic, political, and environmental factors, as well as larger social, cultural, and historical contexts, affect how people and families grow and change.

Linked Lives

This idea acknowledges the importance of human connections in development and the fact that people are in relationships in which each person's development path affects and is affected by the development paths of others in the relationship.

---

1   It is important to note that all choices are constrained by a variety of factors (James et al., 2018).

Multiple Time Clocks

One basic premise of the life course theory is that there can be multiple time lines within a family that overlap at once and could interact with one another.

Resilience

This concept refers to the ability of individuals and families to adapt and thrive in the face of adversity. Resilience is seen as a key component of family development and can be fostered through supportive relationships, access to resources, and the development of coping strategies.

Considerations for Application

Family life course theory has been used to study a wide range of family-related topics, such as marriage, parenting, grandparenting, youth development, and young adulthood. Here are some examples of how the theory has been applied to these areas:

Marriage

Family life course theory has been used to understand the factors that influence the timing and quality of marital relationships, including the influence of cultural and social norms, economic and educational factors, and individual characteristics such as personality and attachment style (Umberson et al., 2010).

Using data from the National Longitudinal Survey of Youth, Arocho and Dush (2020) examined factors (e.g., poverty, family structure, religion, premarital childbearing, cohabitation) that influence desires to meet marital timing desires by age 40. Overall, education and religiosity appeared to delay marriage; however, a variety of factors contributed to whether and when desired marriage plans materialized.

Siblings

Life course has also been used to study sibling relationships. White (2004) found that sibling relationships change a lot in early adulthood. However, proximity and contact stabilize in middle age and rarely change anymore. After about age 70, sibling exchange shows a small increase.

Parenting

Family life course theory has been used to understand the ways in which parenting practices and strategies change over time as children grow and develop. Umberson and Gove (1989) note that the theory emphasizes the importance of understanding the impact of transitions, such as the birth of a child, on parental roles and relationships.

Fathering

One of the most comprehensive applications of life course theory to family life was a paper authored by Kevin Roy (2014). This report provides some clarity as to how life course theory has been used to study fathering and some suggestions for how scholars can better understand the experience of fathering through a variety of life course concepts.

Grandparenting

Family life course theory has been used to explore the changing roles and relationships of grandparents over time, and the ways in which these changes are influenced by social and cultural factors. The theory highlights the importance of understanding the impact of transitions, such as the birth of a grandchild or the death of a spouse, on grandparenting roles and relationships (Hagestad, 1988; Hagestad & Burton, 1986).

Youth Development

Family life course theory has been used to understand the ways in which family dynamics and relationships influence the development of children and adolescents over time. The theory stresses how important it is to understand how changes like divorce or remarriage affect the development and adjustment of young people (Elder & Conger, 2000).

Young Adulthood

Family life course theory has been used to understand the challenges and opportunities faced by young adults as they navigate the transition to adulthood. The theory stresses how important it is to understand how family relationships and experiences affect the development of young adults, including how family support and resources can help or hurt a young person's transition to adulthood (Arnett, 2000).

Conclusion

Family life course theory is a way to understand how family relationships change over time. The theory stresses how important it is to understand how family experiences and changes, like getting married, having kids, and getting older, affect a person's development and well-being. Family life course theory helps us understand the different experiences families have at different times in their lives by looking at how family relationships and the social environment interact.

Discussion Questions

1. How might the principles of family life course theory apply to your own family experiences and transitions?
2. What are some of the strengths and limitations of family life course theory in terms of its ability to explain family development over time?
3. How might family life course theory inform interventions or policies designed to support families through challenging transitions or life events?
4. How might future research further refine and expand our understanding of family life course theory?
5. What are some potential implications of family life course theory for the broader field of family science and related disciplines?

References

Arnett, J. J. (2000). Emerging adulthood: A theory of development from the late teens through the twenties. *American Psychologist, 55*(5), 469–480.

Arocho, R., & Kamp Dush, C. M. (2020). "Best-laid plans": Barriers to meeting marital timing desires over the life course. *Marriage & Family Review, 56*(7), 633–656.

Bengtson, V. L., & Allen, K. R. (1993). The life course perspective applied to families over time. In P. G. Boss, W. J. Doherty, R. LaRossa, W. R. Schumm, & S. K. Steinmetz (Eds.), *Sourcebook of family theories and methods: A contextual approach* (pp. 469–498). Plenum Press.

De Jong, G. F., & Graefe, D. R. (2008). Family life course transitions and the economic consequences of internal migration. *Population, Space and Place, 14*(4), 267–282.

Elder Jr, G. H. (1998). The life course as developmental theory. *Child development, 69*(1), 1–12. https://doi.org/10.1111/j.1467-8624.1998.tb06128.x

Elder, G. H., & Conger, R. D. (2000). *Children of the land: Adversity and success in rural America.* University of Chicago Press.

Elder, G. H., Johnson, M. K., & Crosnoe, R. (2003). The emergence and development of life course theory. In J. T. Mortimer & M. J. Shanahan (Eds.), *Handbook of the life course* (pp. 3–19). Kluwer Academic.

Greenfield, E. A., & Marks, N. F. (2006). Linked lives: Adult children's problems and their parents' psychological and relational well-being. *Journal of Marriage and Family, 68*(2), 442–454. https://doi.org/10.1111%2Fj.1741-3737.2006.00263.x

Gilligan, M., Karraker, A., & Jasper, A. (2018). Linked lives and cumulative inequality: A multigenerational family life course framework. *Journal of Family Theory & Review, 10*(1), 111–125. https://doi.org/10.1111/jftr.12244

Hagestad, G. O. (1988). Demographic change and the life course: Some emerging trends in the family realm. *Family Relations, 37*(4), 405–410. https://doi.org/10.2307/584111

Hagestad, G. O., & Burton, L. M. (1986). Grandparenthood, life context, and family development. *American Behavioral Scientist, 29*(4), 471–484.

James, A. G., Coard, S. I., Fine, M. A., & Rudy, D. (2018). The central roles of race and racism in reframing family systems theory: A consideration of choice and time. *Journal of Family Theory & Review, 10*(2), 419–433. https://doi.org/10.1111/jftr.12262

Macmillan, R., & Copher, R. (2005). Families in the life course: Interdependency of roles, role configurations, and pathways. *Journal of Marriage and Family, 67*(4), 858–879. https://doi.org/10.1111/j.1741-3737.2005.00180.x

McGoldrick, M., Preto, N. A. G., & Carter, B. A. (2013). *The expanded family life cycle: Individual, family, and social perspectives: Pearson new international edition.* Pearson Higher Ed.

Roy, K. (2014). Fathering from the long view: Framing personal and social change through life course theory. *Journal of Family Theory & Review, 6*(4), 319–335. https://doi.org/10.1111/jftr.12050

Thornton, A., & Lin, H. S. (1994). *Social change and the family in Taiwan.* University of Chicago Press.

Thornton, A., & Fricke, T. E. (1987, September). Social change and the family: Comparative perspectives from the West, China, and South Asia. In *Sociological forum* (Vol. 2, No. 4, pp. 746–779). Dordrecht: Kluwer Academic Publishers.

Umberson, D., & Gove, W. R. (1989). Parenthood and psychological well-being: Theory, measurement, and stage in the family life course. *Journal of Family Issues, 10*(4), 440–462.

Umberson, D., Pudrovska, T., & Reczek, C. (2010). Parenthood, childlessness, and well-being: A life course perspective. *Journal of Marriage and Family, 72*(3), 612–629. https://doi.org/10.1111/j.1741-3737.2010.00721.x

Wallerstein, J. S. (1991). The long-term effects of divorce on children: A review. *Journal of the American Academy of Child & Adolescent Psychiatry, 30*(3), 349–360. https://doi.org/10.1097/00004583-199105000-00001

Wallerstein, J. S., & Lewis, J. M. (2004). The unexpected legacy of divorce: Report of a 25-year study. *Psychoanalytic Psychology, 21*(3), 353. https://psycnet.apa.org/doi/10.1037/0736-9735.21.3.353

White, L. (2004). Sibling relationships over the life course: A panel analysis. *Journal of Marriage and Family, 63*(2), 555–568. https://doi.org/10.1111/j.1741-3737.2001.00555.x

CHAPTER 10

Family Stress Theory

Basic premise	
Key figures	
Epistemology	
Assumptions	
Concepts	
Level of analysis	
Relevant studies	

Theory Overview

As per the goal of the text outlined in the preface, this is a general overview of family stress theory. This overview focuses on explaining the theory in a way that helps professionals who work with families, like family scientists, do their jobs better. After the theory is explained, some considerations for practice are given to help the theory be used in a variety of situations.

The World Health Organization (WHO, 2023) defines stress as a state of worry or mental tension caused by a difficult situation that forces people to address the problems that threaten their lives. Importantly, the WHO also notes that stress is not all negative in that appropriate amounts of stress can motivate people to help them perform their daily activities. However, too much stress can overwhelm the resources available to individuals, which can result in a variety of negative outcomes.

The WHO approaches stress from an individual standpoint. Given the family focus of this text, this chapter focuses on how groups we define as families experience and respond to stress.

Basic Premise

Understanding family stress is critical to successfully engaging families because family stress is universal in that all families must navigate stress (James et al., 2020). Though families may experience stress in different ways and/or at different times, no human family can escape stress because life places demands on individuals and families that require them to respond.

The cornerstone of family stress theory is that all families experience stressors, and how families respond to stress varies across time and place. Additionally, how families cope with stress affects their overall well-being. Family stress theory says that things like money problems or illness can upset the balance of a family system and cause tension between family members. How a family copes with stress depends on a variety of factors, including the availability of resources, the nature of the stressor, and the family's coping skills.

Family stress can be traced to both outside and inside factors, such as changes in family structure, financial stress, and the way the family works, which can result in positive results (e.g., effectively addressing the demand that is creating the stress) or negative outcomes, such as increased or continued family conflict, depression, and poor physical health. Family stress theory says that families can effectively respond to stress by managing their resources (Bush & Price, 2020; Cohen & Strong, 2020; Coyne & Padilla-Walker, 2014).

Family stress theory is based on several key assumptions about families, stress, and coping (Patterson, 1988; Walsh, 2003, 2012), which are critical to understanding and addressing stress in family life.

Stress is a Constant in Family Life

One of the central assumptions of family stress theory is that stress is a normal and predictable part of family life. This means that families will inevitably experience stressors, such as illness, financial problems, or interpersonal conflict, and that these stressors can disrupt the equilibrium (read: balance) of the family system.

Families have the Capacity to be Resilient in the Face of Stressful Circumstances

Another key assumption of family stress theory is that families are resilient and have the capacity to adapt to stress. This means that families are not passive victims of stress but rather active agents who can mobilize resources and coping strategies to manage stress and maintain their well-being.

There is Variation in Family Responses to Stress

Family stress theory assumes that how families cope with stress depends on a variety of factors, including the nature of the stressor, the resources available to the family, and the family's coping skills. For example, families may cope with stress by seeking social support, using problem-solving skills, or engaging in religious or spiritual practices (Chatters & Taylor, 2005).

Family stress theory is based on a concept called "social constructionism," which says that language, communication, and culture all play a role in how we understand the world (Gergen, 1992). According to this point of view, our interactions and conversations with other people, as well as our culture and history, all influence what we know about family stress and how to deal with it. Family stress is not an objective, universal thing. Instead, it is a particular and individual experience that depends on how people and their families perceive and comprehend their experiences (Boss, 1987, pp. 695–723; Hill, 1958; McCubbin et al., 1980).

The intellectual roots of family stress theory propose that family members engage in a process of meaning-making in response to stressors, which involves interpreting the stressor, assessing its significance and impact on the family, and formulating coping strategies. From a social constructionist point of view, it's also important to look at family stress and ways to deal with it in a holistic and systemic way (Bush & Price, 2020; Hill, 1958). This approach recognizes that family members are interconnected and that stress in one part of the system can affect other parts of the system. So, interventions and support should take into account the needs of the whole family and focus on making the family stronger and giving them more ways to address challenges (Bush & Price, 2020; Zalaquett & Wood, 1998).

Key Figures

Family stress theory has been developed and expanded upon by a number of scholars in various disciplines, including family science, psychology, and sociology. Some of the key figures in family stress theory include:

Reuben (1949; 1958) developed the ABC-X model of family stress, which proposes that stress is a function of the interaction between the stressor, the family's resources and coping strategies, and the family's perception and appraisal of the stressor. His work emphasized the importance of understanding the subjective experience of stress in families. Pauline (1987) is known for her work on ambiguous loss, a type of stressor that involves loss or change that is unclear or uncertain. Her work emphasizes the importance of maintaining a sense of hope and resilience in the face of ambiguous loss. Harold and Margaret McCubbin and colleagues (1997) developed the resiliency model of family stress, adjustment, and adaptation, which proposes that families have the capacity to adapt and thrive in the face of stress. Their model emphasizes the importance of family resources, coping strategies, and communication in promoting resilience. Ann (2015) conducted extensive research on resilience in children and families. Her work emphasizes the importance of protective factors, such as social support, adaptive coping skills, and positive family relationships, in promoting resilience in the face of stress.

Overall, the major contributors to FST have helped to shape the theory and its application in research and practice. Their contributions have allowed for a more comprehensive understanding of how family dynamics and environmental stressors can influence individual and family functioning.

Key Concepts

Family stress theory is based on several key concepts that help explain how families experience and cope with stress. These concepts include stressors, resources, coping strategies, and adaptation (Adamson et al., 2022; Alianiello, 2005; Henderson & Allen, 2016; Masten & Monn, 2015; Pearlin, 1989; Smith & Landoor, 2018).

Stressors

Stressors are events or situations that disrupt the equilibrium of the family system, such as illness, financial problems, or interpersonal conflict. According to family stress theory, stress is a normal and predictable part of family life, and families will inevitably experience stressors.

Resources
Resources refer to the assets or strengths that families can draw upon to cope with stressors. These resources can be internal (such as individual or family-level coping skills) or external (such as social support or financial resources). Of note, resources have qualities of scarcity and alternative use, which compounds family stress.

Coping Strategies
Coping strategies are the behaviors or actions that families use to manage stressors. Coping strategies can be problem-focused (such as seeking information or taking action to address the stressor) or emotion-focused (such as seeking social support or engaging in relaxation techniques). The two can also work in tandem with, or sequentially with, each other.

Adaptation
Adaptation refers to the ways in which families change or adjust in response to stressors. According to family stress theory, families have the capacity to adapt and thrive in the face of stress, and the ability to adapt depends on a variety of factors, including the nature of the stressor, the resources available to the family, and the family's coping skills.

Chronic and Acute Stress
Stress can present in families as a lasting or continuous feature or as a temporary or occasional event. For instance, families that include members with a serious illness may continually experience chronic stress as a result of having to navigate the illness of the family member. Other stressful events are acute (e.g., a car accident) and occur rarely.

On-Time and Off-Time Stress
Families typically develop over time in a patterned and normative manner, within a given context. These shared familial experiences can bring about predictable or expected stressful events (e.g., the birth of children, families adjusting to members transitioning to new developmental stages, preparing for family holiday gatherings), but other stressful events can occur in families that violate the norms and expected patterns of life. One example of this is when a child dies before their parents when the expected pattern is for parents to die before their children.

Family Resilience
Family resilience is the ability of a family to cope with and adapt to stressors in a healthy and positive way.

Considerations for Application

Before putting the theory into practice, it's important to talk about some of the most important models in the family stress theory literature. Each is presented in turn, prior to applying the concepts of family stress theory to aspects of family life (Bush & Price, 2020).

ABC-X Model

The ABC-X is a primary model for studying stress in family life. Reuben Hill (1949) created the ABC-X model of family stress theory, and family stress research has since extensively used and improved upon it. The model proposes that family stress is a function of the interaction between

> A: the stressor event,
>
> B: the family's resources and coping strategies,
>
> C: the family's perception and appraisal of the stressor, and
>
> X: which together determine the level of stress experienced by the family.

Further, the model suggests that the family's perception and appraisal of the stressor is the key factor in determining the level of stress experienced and that this appraisal is influenced by a variety of factors, including the family's beliefs and values, the nature of the stressor event, and the family's previous experiences with stress. The model also emphasizes the importance of the family's resources and coping strategies in mitigating the effects of stressors.

Double ABC-X

The double ABC-X model of family stress theory is an expanded version of the original ABC-X model, which was proposed by McCubbin and Patterson (1983). The model adds an additional layer of complexity to the original model by accounting for ongoing stress and the potential for post-traumatic growth following a stressor event.

In the double ABC-X model, the original ABC-X formula is applied to both the initial stressor event and the ongoing stress, resulting in four key components:

> A1: The initial stressor event
>
> B1: The family's resources and coping strategies in response to the initial stressor
>
> C1: The family's perception and appraisal of the initial stressor
>
> X1: The initial level of stress experienced by the family

Aa: Ongoing stressors that may arise after the initial stressor event

Bb: The family's resources and coping strategies in response to ongoing stress

Cc: The family's perception and appraisal of ongoing stress

Xx: The level of stress experienced by the family in response to ongoing stress

The double ABC-X model also includes a fifth component, which considers the potential for post-traumatic growth, which is the potential for families to experience positive growth and development following a stressor event.

FAAR or Family Adjustment and Adaptation Response

This model has been used to understand how families respond and adapt to stressful situations (Chanda & Alkon, 2018). The FAAR model consist of three domains: demands (sources of stress), mediators (the abilities and resources of the family that can be utilized when navigating stress), and outcomes (the resultant extent to which the family can effectively function after the stress event; also called family functioning or family adaptation).

Mundane Extreme Environmental Stress

This model has been used to understand how Black families understand, define, and respond to the enduring lived experience of navigating race and racism (Peters & Massey, 1983). Importantly, Black families may employ a wide range of responses to such stressors, given that they can range from mundane (for some families) to extreme.

Family stress theory has been widely applied to a variety of contexts and life stages, including marriage, parenting, grandparenting, youth development, and young adulthood. Here are some examples of how family life stress theory has been applied:

Marriage

The impact of job loss on marital satisfaction and communication has been studied using family stress theory (Lavner et al., 2016). The transition to parenthood has been examined using family stress theory to understand the challenges that couples face during this time (Kuersten-Hogan & McHale, 2021).

Parenting

Family stress theory has been used to explore the impact of parenting stress on child development and behavior (Deater-Deckard, 2008; Masarik &

Conger, 2017). The effects of military deployment on parenting and family functioning have been studied using family stress theory (O'Neal et al., 2018).

Grandparenting

Family stress theory has been applied to the study of grandparent caregiving, particularly in cases where grandparents are providing primary care for their grandchildren due to parental substance abuse or incarceration (Sands & Goldberg-Glen, 2000).

Youth Development

Family stress theory has been used to understand the effects of family conflict and stress on adolescent mental health and development (Walsh, 2011). The impact of neighborhood stress on youth development has been studied using family stress theory (Smith et al., 2016).

Young Adulthood

Family stress theory has been applied to the study of emerging adulthood, particularly in terms of how young adults navigate the transition to independent living and establish their own families (Ranta et al., 2020). The impact of family stress on college students' mental health and academic performance has been studied using family stress theory (Li et al., 2019).

Conclusion

Family stress theory provides a useful framework for understanding how families experience stress and how they cope with stressors. This theory suggests that stressors can lead to negative outcomes such as conflict and dysfunction, but families can use coping strategies and social support to manage stress and adapt to changes.

Applications of family stress theory have included research on a variety of stressors and their effects on families, as well as interventions to help families cope with stress. For example, studies have explored how families cope with chronic illness, financial difficulties, and divorce. Interventions based on family stress theory have included family therapy, parent training, and support groups.

Overall, family stress theory has contributed to our understanding of how families navigate stressful situations and how we can support families in managing stress. Future research and interventions can continue to build on this theory to further support families in their efforts to adapt and thrive in the face of stressors.

Discussion Question

1. How does family stress theory explain how families understand and respond to the development of mental health issues in family members?
2. How can family stress theory be used to understand the impact of poverty on family functioning?
3. What are the implications of family stress theory for understanding the effects of trauma on family functioning?
4. What is the difference between the ABC-X and double ABC-X models of family stress?
5. How can family stress theory be used to understand the impact of divorce on family functioning?

References

Adamsons, K., Few-Demo, A. L., Proulx, C. M., & Roy, K. (2022). Family theories and methodologies: A dynamic approach. In *Sourcebook of Family Theories and Methodologies: A Dynamic Approach* (pp. 3–20). Cham: Springer International Publishing.

Alianiello, L. L. (2005). *The resiliency model of family stress, adjustment, and adaptation: A case study* [Master's thesis, Ohio State University]. OhioLINK Electronic Theses and Dissertations Center. http://rave.ohiolink.edu/etdc/view?acc_num=osu1302548745

Boss, P. (1987). Family stress. In M. B. Sussman & S. K. Steinmetz (Eds.), *Handbook of marriage and the family* (pp. 695–723). Plenum Press.

Bush, K. R., & Price, C. A. (Eds.). (2020). *Families & change: Coping with stressful events and transitions*. SAGE Publications.

Chanda, N., Alkon. A. (2018). Use of the family adjustment and adaptation response model to understand the impact of stress in children. *International Journal of Nursing and Health Care Research*, https://doi.org/10.29011/ IJNHR-155. 100055

Chatters, L. M., & Taylor, R. J. (2005). Religion and families. In V. L. Bengtson, A. C. Acock, K. R. Allen, P. Dilworth-Anderson, & D. M. Klein (Eds.), *Sourcebook of family theory & research* (pp. 517–541). SAGE Publications. https://doi.org/10.4135/9781412990172.n21

Cohen, T. F., & Strong, B. (2020). *The marriage and family experience: Intimate relationships in a changing society*. Cengage Learning.

Coyne, S. M., Padilla-Walker, L. M., Fraser, A. M., Fellows, K., & Day, R. D. (2014). "Media time = family time" positive media use in families with adolescents. *Journal of Adolescent Research*, 29(5), 663–688. https://doi.org/10.1177/0743558414538316

Deater-Deckard, K. (2008). *Parenting stress*. Yale University Press.

Gergen, K. J. (1992). The social constructionist movement in modern psychology. In R. B. Miller (Ed.), *The restoration of dialogue: Readings in the philosophy of clinical psychology* (pp. 556–569). American Psychological Association. https://doi.org/10.1037/10112-044

Henderson, A. C., & Allen, K. R. (2016). *Family theories: Foundations and applications.* Wiley-Blackwell.

Hill, R. (1958). 1. Generic features of families under stress. *Social Casework, 39*(2–3), 139–150.

James, A. G., Barrios, V. R., Roy, R., & Lee, S. (2020). Race, Ethnicity, and Family Stress. In. K. R. Bush & C. A. Price's (Eds.), *Families & change: Coping with stressful events and transitions* (6th ed., pp. 283–304). SAGE Publications.

Kuersten-Hogan, R., McHale, J.P. (2021). The transition to parenthood: A theoretical and empirical overview. In R. Kuersten-Hogan & J. P. McHale (Eds.), *Prenatal family dynamics.* Springer. https://doi.org/10.1007/978-3-030-51988-9_1

Li, M., Li, W. Q., & Li, L. M. W. (2019). Sensitive periods of moving on mental health and academic performance among university students. *Frontiers in Psychology, 10,* 1289. https://doi.org/10.3389/fpsyg.2019.01289

Lavner, J. A., Karney, B. R., & Bradbury, T. N. (2016). "Does couples' communication predict marital satisfaction, or does marital satisfaction predict communication?" *Journal of Marriage and Family, 78*(3), 680–694. https://doi.org/10.1111/jomf.12301

Masarik, A. S., & Conger, R. D. (2017). Stress and child development: A review of the family stress model. *Current Opinion in Psychology, 13,* 85–90. https://doi.org/10.1016/j.copsyc.2016.05.008

Masten, A. S., & Monn, A. R. (2015). Child and family resilience: A call for integrated science, practice, and professional training. *Family Relations, 64*(1), 5–21. https://doi.org/10.1111/fare.12103

Masten, A. S. (2015). *Ordinary magic: Resilience in development.* Guilford Publications.

McCubbin, H. I., & Patterson, J. M. (1983). The family stress process: The double ABCX model of adjustment and adaptation. *Marriage & Family Review, 6*(1–2), 7–37. https://doi.org/10.1300/J002v06n01_02

McCubbin, H. I., McCubbin, M. A., Thompson, A. I., Sae-Young, H., & Allen, C. T. (1997). Families under stress: What makes them resilient. *Journal of family and Consumer Sciences, 89*(3), 2.

McCubbin, H. I., Joy, C. B., Cauble, A. E., Comeau, J. K., Patterson, J. M., & Needle, R. H. (1980). Family stress and coping: A decade review. *Journal of Marriage and the Family, 42*(4), 855–871.

O'Neal, C. W., Lucier-Greer, M., Duncan, J. M., Mallettee, J. K., Arnold, L., & Mancini, J. A. (2018). Vulnerability and resilience within military families: Deployment experiences, reintegration, and family functioning. *Journal of Child and Family Studies, 27,* 3250–3261. https://doi.org/10.1007/s10826-018-1149-6

Patterson, J. M. (1988). Families experiencing stress: I. The family adjustment and adaptation response model: II. Applying the FAAR Model to health-related issues for intervention and research. *Family Systems Medicine, 6*(2), 202.

Pearlin, L. I. (1989). The sociological study of stress. *Journal of Health and Social Behavior, 30*(3), 241–256. https://doi.org/10.2307/2136956

Peters, M. F., & Massey, G. (1983). Mundane extreme environmental stress in family stress theories: The case of black families in white America. *Marriage & Family Review, 6*(1–2), 193–218. https://doi.org/10.1300/J002v06n01_10

Ranta, M., Punamäki, R. L., Chow, A., & Salmela-Aro, K. (2020). The economic stress model in emerging adulthood: The role of social relationships and financial capability. *Emerging Adulthood, 8*(6), 496–508. https://doi.org/10.1177/2167696819893574

Sands, R. G., & Goldberg-Glen, R. S. (2000). Factors associated with stress among grandparents raising their grandchildren. *Family Relations, 49*(1), 97–105. https://doi.org/10.1111/j.1741-3729.2000.00097.x

Smith, E. P., Faulk, M., & Sizer, M. A. (2016). Exploring the meso-system: The roles of community, family, and peers in adolescent delinquency and positive youth development. *Youth & Society, 48*(3), 318–343. https://doi.org/10.1177/0044118X13491581

Walsh, F. (2003). Family resilience: A framework for clinical practice. *Family Process, 42*(1), 1–18. https://doi.org/10.1111/j.1545-5300.2003.00001.x

Walsh, F. (2011). Facilitating family resilience: Relational resources for positive youth development in conditions of adversity. In M. Ungar (Ed.), *The social ecology of resilience: A handbook of theory and practice* (pp. 173–185). Springer.

Walsh, F. (2012). Family resilience: Strengths forged through adversity. In F. Walsh (Ed.), *Normal family processes: Growing diversity and complexity* (pp. 399–427). Guildford Press.

World Health Organization. (2023 February 21). *Stress. What is stress?* https://www.who.int/news-room/questions-and-answers/item/stress#:~:text=What%20is%20stress%3F,and%20threats%20in%20our%20lives

Zalaquett, C. P., & Wood, R. J. E. (1998). *Evaluating stress: A book of resources*, Vol. 2. Scarecrow Education.

CHAPTER 11

Symbolic Interactionism

Basic premise	
Key figures	
Epistemology	
Assumptions	
Concepts	
Level of analysis	
Relevant studies	

Theory Overview

Per the goal of the text outlined in the preface, this is a general overview of symbolic interactionism theory. This overview focuses on presenting the theory to the extent that it equips professionals who engage families (e.g., family scientists). Following the presentation of the theory, some considerations for practice are offered for application across various levels of context.

Basic Premise

Symbolic interaction theory is a sociological perspective that emphasizes the importance of symbols and their meanings in human social interactions.[1] According to this theory, people create and communicate meaning through symbols, such as language, gestures, and other forms of nonverbal communication. The basic premise of symbolic interaction theory is that individuals construct their social reality through shared meanings and understandings that are negotiated in everyday interactions (Blumer, 1969).

Symbolic interaction theory has been applied to multiple levels of context, including the study of gender, race, and social class. It has also been used to analyze the role of symbols and communication in organizations, the media, and other social institutions (Blumer, 1969).

The epistemology of symbolic interaction theory is based on the idea that knowledge is socially constructed through the use of symbols, language, and communication through ongoing social interactions, which allow for the creation and interpretation of meaning in their social worlds through ongoing interactions with others (Oliver, 2012; Rock, 2016). The emphasis on social construction and interpretation distinguishes symbolic interaction theory from other, more positivist approaches to knowledge generation. Symbolic interaction theory is grounded in the philosophical tradition of pragmatism, which emphasizes the practical consequences of beliefs and actions. Pragmatism rejects the notion of absolute truth and instead focuses on the usefulness of knowledge and ideas in guiding action and solving problems (Caulley, 2007; Mead, 1934).

Symbolic interaction theory is based on several key assumptions about human behavior and social interaction. These assumptions are the foundation of the theory and provide the framework for understanding how individuals create and maintain meaning in their social (Blumer, 1969; Caulley, 2007; Mead, 1934). Aldiabat and Navenec (2011) provided several assumptions of the theory, highlighting the importance of communication and interaction in

---

1   Aldibat and Navenec (2011) define social interaction as "social interaction can be defined as a method that forms and expresses human behaviour" (p. 1065).

shaping individuals' perceptions of the world around them. The assumptions emphasize the importance of language, symbols, and other forms of communication in creating and maintaining social reality.

- Humans act toward things on the basis of the meanings they ascribe to those things.
- Meaning arises from social interaction with others.
- Meanings are modified through an interpretive process that occurs in response to ongoing interaction.
- The interpretation of symbols is modified by an individual's own thought processes.
- Symbolic interaction is a process of ongoing interpretation.

Key Figures

The theory was first developed by George Herbert Mead in the early 20th century and has since been elaborated on by many other sociologists, including Herbert Blumer and Erving Goffman. Mead's work emphasized the role of language and communication in shaping social reality, while Blumer focused on the importance of social interaction in the construction of meaning. Goffman's work examined the ways in which individuals present themselves in social situations and everyday life and the impact of these presentations on others (Blumer, 1980; Goffman 1959; Scheff, 2005; Turner, 2012).

Key Concepts

Symbolic interaction theory is based on several key concepts that provide a framework for understanding human behavior and social interaction (Aldiabat & Navenec, 2011). These concepts are central to the theory and emphasize the importance of communication, symbols, and interpretation in shaping social reality.

The Self

The self refers to an individual's sense of identity and personal agency. Components of the self include aspects that are instinctual and respond to others in an impulsive and unorganized manner (referred to as the "I"), with the other component being the aspect of the self that consists of a more coordinated and organized response that fits within expected social norms (referred to as the "Me"). Both contribute to "the self," which is shaped by social interaction and is constantly evolving through ongoing communication and interpretation.

Symbols (Sometimes also Referred to as Objects)

A symbol is any object, gesture, word, or image that is used to represent something else. Any entity of the human lived experience that can be "indicated ... pointed to ... or referred to" (Blumer, 1969, p. 10). These can be living or nonliving entities that guide or shape human interactions. Thus, humans regularly ascribe meaning to objects, which guides the way the person (read: their self) responds (read: I or me) to the object. Symbols are a fundamental component of human communication and are essential for the creation and interpretation of meaning.

Meaning

Meaning refers to the significance that individuals attach to symbols and objects. This significance is created and modified through ongoing social interaction and interpretation. The interpretation is the process of assigning meaning to symbols. This process is ongoing and is shaped by an individual's past experiences, cultural background, and social context. In other words, the meaning of symbols can change over the course of time and/or place.

Role-Taking

Humans engage in a process of imagining the *self* as seen from the standpoint of others in society (also referred to as the generalized other). Mead defined the generalized other as "the organized community or social group which gives the individual his unity of self" (Mead, 1934, p. 154). Importantly, the generalized other can be a single individual or group(s) of others.

Looking-Glass Self

Another prominent symbolic interactionist theorist was Charles Cooley. He coined this term to better understand how humans develop. While Mead focused on the generalized other, Cooley (1902) described how people defined the self in a different manner. Aldiabat and Navenec (2011) perfectly describe Cooley's perspective:

> Cooley suggested that human beings define and develop themselves in every situation as a result of imaginative processes and emotions to reflect attitudes of others through what Cooley called the looking-glass self (p. 1067).

Importantly, each of these concepts contribute not only to understanding how a person develops but also how they are socialized into context-specific cultures and how they learn and internalize the norms, values, and beliefs.

This process is essential for the development of the self and for effective social interaction. One of the primary socializing agents of humans is the family(s) they are connected to.

Considerations for Application

Symbolic interaction theory has been applied to a wide range of topics related to human behavior and social interaction, including marriage, parenting, grandparenting, youth development, and young adulthood, which provides some considerations for how to apply the theory across familial contexts (Laursen & Collins, 2003; Markham et al., 2017; McNaughton & Niedzwiecki, 2000; Stryker, 1972).

Marriage

Symbolic interaction theory has been used to study the process of mate selection and the role of communication in marital relationships. For example, researchers have found that communication patterns, such as the use of positive and negative affect, play a key role in marital satisfaction (Bolton, 1961; Gottman, 2013; Hall, 2022; Zaidi & Shuraydi, 2002).

Parenting

Symbolic interaction theory has been used to study the role of communication in parent-child relationships (Putallaz & Heflin, 1990). Researchers have found that parent-child communication is essential for the development of the child's sense of self and for the formation of close parent-child relationships (Lamb, 2011; Peterson & McCabe, 1994; Wass et al., 2020).

Grandparenting

Symbolic interaction theory has been used to study the role of grandparents in the lives of their grandchildren. Research has shown that grandparent-grandchild relationships are shaped by communication patterns and by the meanings that individuals attach to their roles as grandparents (Reitzes et al., 2004; Silverstein et al., 2003; Taylor et al., 2005).

Youth Development

Symbolic interaction theory has been used to study the role of peer relationships in youth development. Researchers have found that peer communication and interactions play a key role in shaping adolescents' self-concepts and identities (Lyons et al., 2010).

Young Adulthood

Symbolic interaction theory has been used to study the transition to adulthood and the formation of adult identities. Research has shown that communication patterns and social interactions play a key role in shaping individuals' sense of self and in facilitating the transition to adulthood (Côté et al., 2014, 2015; Peterson, 1987).

Conclusion

Symbolic interaction theory offers a compelling lens through which to understand the role of families as valuable symbols and objects critical in the socialization of family members and the development of meaning. By emphasizing the ways in which individuals actively construct and negotiate their understanding of social reality through their interactions with others, this theory highlights how families serve as key sites of socialization, where members learn to interpret and make sense of their world. Moreover, symbolic interaction theory underscores the importance of ongoing communication and interaction in shaping family dynamics and relationships, and in providing opportunities for members to negotiate and reaffirm their shared meanings and values. As such, this theory provides a powerful framework for understanding the critical role of families in the development of individual identity and the maintenance of social order, and offers important insights for practitioners and researchers seeking to support healthy and thriving family relationships.

Discussion Questions

1. How might the principles of symbolic interaction theory apply to your own experiences in your family of origin or your current family?
2. What are some of the benefits and limitations of using symbolic interaction theory as a framework for understanding family life?
3. In what ways might families serve as valuable symbols and objects in the socialization of family members and the development of meaning, as described by symbolic interaction theory?
4. How might the principles of symbolic interaction theory apply to the experiences of families from different cultural or socioeconomic backgrounds?
5. Can you think of any examples from popular media or literature that illustrate the principles of symbolic interaction theory as they relate to family dynamics?

6. In what ways might symbolic interaction theory be used to inform family therapy or other forms of intervention for families experiencing challenges or conflicts?

References

Aldiabat, K. M., & Navenec, L. (2011). Philosophical roots of classical grounded theory: Its foundations in symbolic interactionism. *Qualitative Report, 16*(4), 1063–1080. https://files.eric.ed.gov/fulltext/EJ940800.pdf

Blumer, H. (1969). *Symbolic interactionism: Perspective and method.* University of California Press.

Blumer, H. (1980). Mead and Blumer: The convergent methodological perspectives of social behaviorism and symbolic interactionism. *American Sociological Review, 45*(3), 409–419.

Bolton, C. D. (1961). Mate selection as the development of a relationship. *Marriage and Family Living, 23*(3), 234–240. https://doi.org/10.2307/346967

Caulley, D. N. (2007). Symbolic interactionism: An introduction, an interpretation, an integration. *Qualitative Research Journal, 6*(2), 225–227.

Cooley, C. H. (1902). *Human nature and the social order.* Charles Scribner's Sons.

Côté, J. E., & Levine, C. G. (2014). *Identity, formation, agency, and culture: A social psychological synthesis.* Psychology Press.

Côté, J. E., & Levine, C. (2015). *Identity formation, youth, and development: A simplified approach.* Psychology Press.

Gottman, J. M. (2013). *Marital interaction: Experimental investigations.* Elsevier.

Hall, S. (2022). Application: Symbolic interactionism as a framework for marital meaning. In K. Adamsons, A. L. Few-Demo, C. M. Proulx, & K. Roy's, *Sourcebook of family theories and methodologies: A dynamic approach* (pp. 147–154). Springer International Publishing.

Lamb, M. E. (Ed.). (2011). The role of parent-child relationships in child development. In M. H. Bornstein & M. E. Lamb (Eds.), *Developmental science: An advanced textbook* (pp. 469–517). Psychology Press.

Laursen, B., & Collins, W. A. (2003). Parent-child communication during adolescence. In A. L. Vangelisti *The Routledge handbook of family communication* (pp. 357–372). Routledge.

Lyons, H., Giordano, P. C., Manning, W. D., & Longmore, M. A. (2010). Identity, peer relationships, and adolescent girls' sexual behavior: An exploration of the contemporary double standard. *Journal of Sex Research, 48*(5), 437–449. https://doi.org/10.1080/00224499.2010.506679

Markham, R. L., Cheung Siu, C., Tiffan, N., Kohli, S., & Schieferstein, J. L. (2017). *Phone home: Parent-child support in college students' social interaction.* Cedarville University.

McNaughton, J., & Niedzwiecki, C. K. (2000). Gender differences in parent child communication patterns. *Journal of Undergraduate Research*, *3*, 25–32.

Mead, G. H. (1934). *Mind, self, and society* (Vol. 111). University of Chicago Press.

Oliver, C. (2012). The relationship between symbolic interactionism and interpretive description. *Qualitative Health Research*, *22*(3), 409–415. https://doi.org/10.1177/1049732311421177

Peterson, C., & McCabe, A. (1994). A social interactionist account of developing decontextualized narrative skill. *Developmental Psychology*, *30*(6), 937. https://journals.sagepub.com/doi/pdf/10.1177/074355488723005

Peterson, G. W. (1987). Role transitions and role identities during adolescence: A symbolic interactionist view. *Journal of Adolescent Research*, *2*(3), 237–254.

Putallaz, M., & Heflin, A. H. (1990). Parent-child interaction. In S. R. Asher & J. D. Coie (Eds.), *Peer Rejection in Childhood* (p. 189). Cambridge University Press.

Reitzes, D. C., & Mutran, E. J. (2004). Grandparenthood: Factors influencing frequency of grandparent—grandchildren contact and grandparent role satisfaction. *The Journals of Gerontology Series B: Psychological Sciences and Social Sciences*, *59*(1), S9–S16. https://doi.org/10.1093/geronb/59.1.S9

Rock, P. (2016). *Making of symbolic interactionism*. Springer.

Scheff, T. J. (2005). Looking-glass self: Goffman as symbolic interactionist. *Symbolic Interaction*, *28*(2), 147–166. https://doi.org/10.1525/si.2005.28.2.147

Silverstein, M., Giarrusso, R., & Bengtson, V. L. (2003). Grandparents and grandchildren in family systems: A social-developmental perspective. *Global Aging and Challenges to Families*, 75–102.

Stryker, S. (1972). Symbolic interaction theory: A review and some suggestions for comparative family research. *Journal of Comparative Family Studies*, *3*(1), 17–32. https://doi.org/10.3138/jcfs.3.1.17

Taylor, A. C., Robila, M., & Lee, H. S. (2005). Distance, contact, and intergenerational relationships: Grandparents and adult grandchildren from an international perspective. *Journal of Adult Development*, *12*, 33–41. https://doi.org/10.1007/s10804-005-1280-7

Turner, J. H. (2012). *Theoretical sociology: 1830 to the present*. SAGE Publications.

Wass, S. V., Whitehorn, M., Haresign, I. M., Phillips, E., & Leong, V. (2020). Interpersonal neural entrainment during early social interaction. *Trends in Cognitive Sciences*, *24*(4), 329–342. https://doi.org/10.1016/j.tics.2020.01.006

Zaidi, A. U., & Shuraydi, M. (2002). Perceptions of arranged marriages by young Pakistani Muslim women living in a Western society. *Journal of Comparative Family Studies*, *33*(4), 495–514. https://doi.org/10.3138/jcfs.33.4.495

CHAPTER 12

Attachment Theory

Basic premise	
Key figures	
Epistemology	
Assumptions	
Concepts	
Level of analysis	
Relevant studies	

Theory Overview

Per the goal of the text outlined in the preface, this is a general overview of attachment theory. This overview focuses on presenting the theory to the extent that it equips professionals who engage families (e.g., family scientists). Following the presentation of the theory, some considerations for practice are offered for application across various levels of context.

Basic Premise

Attachment theory is a psychological model that attempts to describe the dynamics of long-term and short-term interpersonal relationships between humans. It is a theory of relationships between individuals, focusing on the emotional bonds between people. The most important tenet of attachment theory is that an infant needs to develop a relationship with at least one primary caregiver for social and emotional development to occur normally (Ainsworth, 1973; Bowlby, 1969). Attachment theory posits that this relationship acts as a prototype for all future social relationships, serving as a blueprint for how the individual will interact with others throughout life. Attachment theory has been applied to a variety of contexts, including parent-child relationships, romantic relationships, and friendships (Mikulincer & Shaver, 2007). Van Vuuren (2007) lists the epistemology of attachment theory as intersubjective. Specifically, intersubjectivity in terms of the connection between the individuals and their caregiver, and how that context sets the foundation and pathway for attachments and detachments the person experiences throughout the life course.

John Bowlby (1969, 1973), the main architect of attachment theory, articulated several assumptions of the theory. First, he noted that attachment behavior is built into the DNA of the human species, which increases the chances of survival of its young. Specifically, caregivers take on the role and responsibility of protecting and meeting the needs of children, which helps them adapt and survive their environment. Second, confidence in a caregiver meeting one's needs reduces the anxieties and fears of the young person. Thus, the more that a caregiver fails at meeting the needs of the young person, the lower the results in confidence and increased fears and anxiety. Third, the internalization of attachment behaviors is developed early in life and sets the stage for how one connects to others throughout their life course. Fourth, the development of attachment behaviors occurs through actual experiences with caregivers. The extent to which caregivers are accessible and responsive to the child's needs helps the child develop beliefs about how others may or may not meet their emotional needs. These internal expectations continue throughout the life course and extend to all intimate relationships the person experiences (Shaver & Mikulincer, 2005).

Key Figures

John Bowlby (1969) is widely considered to be the founder of attachment theory. He argued that the bond between an infant and its primary caregiver is an important factor in the child's development. Bowlby suggested that the attachment relationship serves as a prototype for all future social relationships.

Mary Ainsworth (1978) was a student of Bowlby's and is credited with furthering the development of attachment theory. She developed the "Strange Situation" experiment, which was used to measure the quality of an infant's attachment to its primary caregiver. Ainsworth identified three distinct attachment styles: secure, avoidant, and ambivalent.

Colwyn Trevarthen (1979, 1998, 1993) was a developmental psychologist who studied the emotional and communicative aspects of the infant-caregiver relationship. He proposed that infants are born with the capacity for communication and that this capacity is essential for the development of secure attachments.

Mary Main (with colleagues, 1985) was a student of Ainsworth's and is credited with introducing the concept of "disorganized attachment." Main argues that some children develop insecure attachments because of inconsistent or unresponsive parenting.

Karen Prager (1995, 1997) was a developmental psychologist who studied the effects of attachment on adult relationships. She proposed that attachment styles developed in childhood can influence adult relationships, and secure attachments are associated with healthier relationships.

Harry Harlow's (1958, 1962, 1965) experiments in the mid-twentieth century revolutionized our understanding of attachment and the social development of infants. His most famous experiments involved rhesus monkeys separated from their mothers and placed in cages with two surrogate mothers. He found that physical touch and comfort were more important to the monkeys' social and emotional development than mere nourishment. His findings have been influential in shaping our understanding of attachment in both human and animal behavior.

Key Concepts

Attachment theory is a psychological model that attempts to describe the dynamics of long-term and short-term interpersonal relationships between humans. It focuses on the emotional bonds between people and the ways in which those bonds are formed, maintained, and changed over time. The main concepts of attachment theory include (Mikulincer & Shaver, 2010; Smith & Hamon, 2022) the following:

Secure Attachment
This is the most common type of attachment, and it occurs when a child feels safe and secure in the presence of their primary caregiver.

Insecure Attachment
This type of attachment occurs when a child does not feel safe or secure in the presence of their primary caregiver.

Attachment Styles
These are the different ways in which people respond to and interact with their primary caregiver.

Attachment Behaviors
These are the behaviors that people use to form and maintain their attachment relationships.

Separation Anxiety
This is the fear or distress that a child experiences when separated from their primary caregiver.

Attachment Theory and Development
This theory suggests that the quality of attachment relationships in early childhood can have an effect on the development of a person's personality and behavior later in life.

Internal Working Models
Internal working models refer to mental representations of attachment relationships that individuals develop based on their early experiences with caregivers. These models consist of beliefs and expectations about the self, others, and the nature of relationships, and they guide behavior in social interactions throughout the life span. Internal working models are thought to be relatively stable and resistant to change, but they can be influenced by new experiences and may shift over time.

Wired to Connect
Refer to the behavioral manifestations of attachment-related behaviors that individuals use to establish and maintain attachment relationships. These wires are seen as biologically based and innate, and they include behaviors such as crying, clinging, and seeking comfort from caregivers. These behaviors are thought to be essential for the development of attachment relationships, as they signal to caregivers the need for support and comfort,

and they establish a foundation of trust and security that underlies the attachment bond.

Considerations for Application

Attachment theory has been applied to a wide range of family relationships, including marriage, parenting, grandparenting, youth development, and young adulthood (Sroufe, 2005). Here are a few examples:

Marriage
Attachment theory has been used to understand the dynamics of romantic relationships, including the ways in which attachment styles can influence relationship satisfaction and stability. Research has focused on how individual attachment styles correlate with relationship success or failure (Furman & Flanagan, 1997; Kotler, 1985).

Parenting
Attachment theory has been applied to understanding parent-child relationships, including the ways in which parenting behaviors can influence attachment patterns (Ainsworth, 1967, 1979). For instance, research has shown that sensitive and responsive parenting can promote secure attachment in infants and young children (Newton, 2008; Palm, 2014; Rholes et al., 1995).

Grandparenting
Attachment theory has also been used to understand the role of grandparents in the lives of their grandchildren. As with parents, research has shown that secure attachment with grandparents can promote positive developmental outcomes for grandchildren (Connor, 2006; Poehlmann 2003).

Youth Development
Attachment theory has been used to understand the factors that promote positive youth development, such as whether and how secure attachment with parents and others can promote resilience and adaptive coping strategies in the face of adversity (Lee & Lok, 2012; Mohamed et al., 2017).

Young Adulthood
Attachment theory has also been applied to understanding the transition to adulthood and the formation of adult romantic relationships. Research has shown that attachment styles can influence the quality of adult romantic relationships and the ability to form lasting, committed partnerships (DiTommaso et al., 2003; Fraley & Davis, 1997).

Conclusion

Attachment theory provides family science with foundational knowledge of the ways in which early experiences with caregivers shape individual beliefs, expectations, and behavior in relationships throughout the lifespan. The concepts of internal working models and wires to connect provide a powerful lens for understanding the cognitive and behavioral mechanisms underlying attachment relationships, and these concepts have been applied to a wide range of family relationships, including marriage, parenting, grandparenting, youth development, and young adulthood. By recognizing the importance of attachment in family relationships and applying the insights of attachment theory, we can promote healthy social and emotional development, strengthen family bonds, and build more fulfilling and satisfying relationships.

Discussion Questions

1. How has your own attachment history influenced your beliefs and expectations about relationships, and how do these beliefs and expectations shape your behavior in your current relationships?
2. How might attachment theory be used to help parents understand and respond to their children's emotional needs?
3. In what ways might attachment theory inform our understanding of intergenerational relationships, such as the relationships between grandparents and grandchildren?
4. How might attachment theory help us understand the challenges and opportunities of romantic relationships, and how might this understanding be used to promote healthy and satisfying partnerships?
5. How might attachment theory be applied in the context of therapy or counseling, and what strategies might be effective for helping individuals develop more secure attachment relationships?

References

Ainsworth, M. S. (1979). Infant–mother attachment. *American Psychologist, 34*(10), 932–937. https://doi.org/10.1037/0003-066X.34.10.932

Ainsworth, M. D. S. (1978). *Patterns of attachment: A psychological study of the strange situation.* Erlbaum.

Ainsworth, M. (1967). Infant-mother attachment. *American Psychologist, 22*(4), 612–619. doi:10.1037/h0024226

Bowlby, J. (1969). *Attachment and loss: Attachment* (Vol. 1). Basic Books.

Bowlby, J. (1973). *Attachment and loss: Separation* (Vol. 2). Basic Books.

Connor, S. (2006). Grandparents raising grandchildren: Formation, disruption and intergenerational transmission of attachment. *Australian Social Work*, *59*(2), 172–184. https://doi.org/10.1080/03124070600651887

DiTommaso, E., Brannen-McNulty, C., Ross, L., & Burgess, M. (2003). Attachment styles, social skills and loneliness in young adults. *Personality and Individual Differences*, *35*(2), 303–312. https://doi.org/10.1016/S0191-8869(02)00190-3

Fraley, R. C., & Davis, K. E. (1997). Attachment formation and transfer in young adults' close friendships and romantic relationships. *Personal Relationships*, *4*(2), 131–144. https://doi.org/10.1111/j.1475-6811.1997.tb00135.x

Furman, W., & Flanagan, A. S. (1997). The influence of earlier relationships on marriage: An attachment perspective. In W. K. Halford & H. J. Markman (Eds.), *Clinical handbook of marriage and couples interventions* (pp. 179–202). John Wiley & Sons, Inc.

Harlow, H. F. (1958). The nature of love. *American Psychologist*, *13*(12), 673.

Harlow, H. F., & Harlow, M. K. (1962). Social deprivation in monkeys. *Scientific American*, *207*(5), 136–150.

Harlow, H. F., Dodsworth, R. O., & Harlow, M. K. (1965). Total social isolation in monkeys. *Proceedings of the National Academy of Sciences*, *54*(1), 90–97.

Kotler, T. (1985). Security and autonomy within marriage. *Human Relations*, *38*(4), 299–321.

Lee, T. Y., & Lok, D. P. (2012). Bonding as a positive youth development construct: A conceptual review. *The Scientific World Journal*. https://doi.org/10.1100/2012/481471

Main, M., Kaplan, N., & Cassidy, J. (1985). Security in infancy, childhood, and adulthood: A move to the level of representation. *Monographs of the Society for Research in Child Development*, *50*(1/2), 66–104. https://doi.org/10.2307/3333827

Mikulincer, M., & Shaver, P. R. (2007). Boosting attachment security to promote mental health, prosocial values, and inter-group tolerance. *Psychological Inquiry*, *18*(3), 139–156.

Mikulincer, M., & Shaver, P. R. (2010). *Attachment in adulthood: Structure, dynamics, and change*. Guilford Publications.

Mohamed, N. H., Hamzah, S. R. A., & Samah, I. A. I. B. A. (2017). Parental and peer attachment and its relationship with positive youth development. *International Journal of Academic Research in Business and Social Sciences*, *7*(9), 352–362.

Newton, R. P. (2008). *The attachment connection: Parenting a secure & confident child using the science of attachment theory*. New Harbinger Publications.

Palm, G. (2014). Attachment theory and fathers: Moving from "being there" to "being with." *Journal of Family Theory & Review*, *6*(4), 282–297. https://doi.org/10.1111/jftr.12045

Poehlmann, J. (2003). An attachment perspective on grandparents raising their very young grandchildren: Implications for intervention and research. *Infant Mental*

Health Journal: Official Publication of the World Association for Infant Mental Health, *24*(2), 149–173. https://doi.org/10.1002/imhj.10047

Rholes, W. S., Simpson, J. A., & Blakely, B. S. (1995). Adult attachment styles and mothers' relationships with their young children. *Personal Relationships*, *2*(1), 35–54. https://doi.org/10.1111/j.1475-6811.1995.tb00076.x

Prager, K. (1995). *Attachment in adulthood: Structure, dynamics, and change*. Guilford Press.

Prager, K. J. (1997). *The psychology of intimacy*. Guilford Press.

Shaver, P. R., & Mikulincer, M. (2005). Attachment theory and research: Resurrection of the psychodynamic approach to personality. *Journal of Research in Personality*, *39*(1), 22–45. https://doi.org/10.1016/j.jrp.2004.09.002

Smith, S., & Hamon, R. (2022). *Exploring family theories*. Oxford University Press.

Sroufe, L. A. (2005). Attachment and development: A prospective, longitudinal study from birth to adulthood. *Attachment & Human Development*, *7*(4), 349–367. https://doi.org/10.1080/14616730500365928

Trevarthen, C. (1979). Communication and cooperation in early infancy. *Before Speech*, 321–347.

Trevarthen, C. (1993). The self born in intersubjectivity: The psychology of an infant communicating. In U. Neisser (Ed.), *The perceived self: Ecological and interpersonal sources of self-knowledge* (pp. 121–173). Cambridge University Press.

Trevarthen, C. (1998). The concept and foundations of infant intersubjectivity. In B. Stein (Ed.), *Intersubjective communication and emotion in early ontogeny* (pp. 15–46). Cambridge University Press.

van Vuuren, R. (2007). *Beyond attachment theory: The hollows and joints of being*. https://www.cirp.uqam.ca/documents%20pdf/Collection%20vol.%201/13.vanVuuren.pdf

CHAPTER 13

Miscellaneous Family Theory Concepts

As noted in the introduction, this text is designed to provide a baseline of knowledge about family theory concepts and their applications. No one text has yet to list all the family theoretical concepts. This one is no different. Therefore, having listed many of the leading theories of family life and relationships in the previous chapters, I briefly review some of the concepts of family life that may come in handy to those interested in studying or engaging families. Though, only as a start. I, again, encourage you to work with your mentor and continue to build your family theory toolkit to develop and maintain deeper knowledge of the subsequent concepts.

Family Resource Management

Family resource management is the study of how families acquire, allocate, and utilize resources to meet their needs and achieve their goals. It involves understanding how families make decisions about time, money, energy, and other resources to maintain their well-being and pursue their aspirations (Moore & Asay, 2017).

The concept of family resource management has been applied in a variety of contexts, including family financial planning, household management, family decision-making, goal setting, time management, and work-family balance. It is also used to examine the ways in which families adapt to changes in their environment, such as economic downturns, technological advances, and social trends. Additional uses include how family resources, including social support and coping strategies, contribute to successful adaptation in children and families. Further, family resource management can be applied to investigate how family resources, such as emotional support and financial stability, affect coping strategies in different demographic groups.

Overall, the study of family resource management is important for understanding how families can effectively manage their resources to improve their well-being and achieve their goals.

Multiple Partner Fertility

Multiple partner fertility (MPF) is a term used in family science to describe the phenomenon of individuals having children with more than one partner (Guzzo, 2014; Monte, 2019). This can occur in a variety of situations, including divorce, separation, or simply having children with different partners over time. MPF has important implications for family dynamics, such as co-parenting, child support, and family relationships. It can also have social and economic consequences, such as poverty, child welfare involvement, and parental stress. This area of research also examines the implications for maternal and child outcomes, as well as how MPF is related to various demographic and socioeconomic factors, and the policies and interventions in place to support families with multiple partner fertility.

Dyadic Adjustment

Dyadic adjustment is a concept in family science that refers to the degree of satisfaction and adjustment in a romantic relationship between two people, often referred to as a dyad (Spanier, 1989). It involves assessing various aspects of the relationship, such as communication, intimacy, shared activities, and conflict resolution, to determine how well the partners are functioning together as a couple. Dyadic adjustment is important for understanding the quality of romantic relationships and how they may impact individual well-being and family dynamics. Poor dyadic adjustment can lead to negative outcomes, such as depression, relationship dissatisfaction, and divorce, while positive dyadic adjustment can lead to improved outcomes, such as marital satisfaction, family stability, and overall well-being. The Dyadic Adjustment Scale is a widely used measure of dyadic adjustment (Graham et al., 2006) and has been quite useful in research and clinical settings.

Family Goal Setting

Family goal setting is a process of identifying, prioritizing, and working toward shared goals among family members (James, 2023 et al., 2019; Rodger et al., 2012). It involves setting objectives that the family as a whole wants to achieve, as well as developing strategies to accomplish them. This concept is important in family science because it helps families work together toward a common purpose, strengthens communication and problem-solving skills, and promotes cohesion and satisfaction. Family goal setting can take many forms, such as financial planning, education, health and wellness, and leisure activities. It can also be used to address specific issues that may arise within the family, such as conflict resolution or coping with a difficult life event.

Marriage, Divorce, and Repartnering

Marriage, divorce, and repartnering are key concepts in family science that relate to the formation, dissolution, and reformation of romantic relationships over time (Coleman & Ganong, 1999; Fine & Harvey, 2013; Sussman et al., 2013). Marriage refers to the legal union between two people, while divorce refers to the legal dissolution of a marriage. Repartnering refers to the process of forming new romantic relationships after the dissolution of a previous relationship, either through remarriage or cohabitation.

These concepts are important in family science because they have significant implications for family dynamics, such as parental and child well-being, family structure and stability, and intergenerational relationships. The study of marriage, divorce, and repartnering can also shed light on broader social and cultural trends, such as changing attitudes toward marriage and family and demographic shifts in the population. This research also explores remarriage and stepfamilies and discusses the various theoretical methods and the importance of understanding the diversity and complexity of remarriage and stepfamilies for future research and intervention.

Dialectical Tensions in Relationships

Dialectical tensions refer to the contradictions and conflicts that arise in close relationships (Baxter, 1990; Baxter et al., 2021), such as family. According to the dialectical perspective, these tensions are an inherent part of all relationships and cannot be entirely eliminated. Instead, individuals and families must learn to manage and balance these tensions to maintain healthy relationships.

Three primary types of dialectical tensions include autonomy/connection, openness/closedness, and predictability/novelty. Autonomy/connection refers to the tension between the desire for independence and the desire for close-ness in relationships. Openness/closedness refers to the tension between the desire for honesty and transparency and the desire for privacy and boundaries. Predictability/novelty refers to the tension between the desire for stability and routine and the desire for spontaneity and excitement.

Examples of dialectical tensions in family relationships include the following:

A married couple may experience autonomy/connection tension when one partner wants to spend more time together while the other wants more space and independence.

A parent and child may experience openness/closedness tension when the child wants to keep a secret from the parent, but the parent values honesty and transparency in their relationship.

A family may experience predictability/novelty tension when one member wants to keep traditions and routines, while another member wants to try new things and have new experiences.

Finally, while these examples show how dialectics work in dyads, it is also possible for dialectical tensions to be present within the individual, where a person in a relationship may experience dialectical tensions within themselves about one of their family relationships.

Generativity

Generativity refers to the concern for future generations and the desire to contribute to the well-being of society beyond one's own personal needs and interests. It is a key aspect of Erik Erikson's (1974) theory of psychosocial development, which suggests that generativity is an important developmental task during midlife. According to Erikson, individuals who achieve genera-tivity experience a sense of satisfaction and fulfillment in their lives, while those who do not may experience a sense of stagnation and unfulfillment. Generativity can be expressed in a variety of ways, including through raising children, mentoring others, contributing to one's community, and engaging in meaningful work.

McAdams (2004) writes that midlife adults were more likely to express generativity than younger or older adults, including members of their own families. Further, generativity is believed to be a key aspect of psychological development during midlife, as individuals begin to shift their focus from personal goals to broader concerns for the future, which certainly includes what they socialize in the younger generations of their family.

Cohabitation

Cohabitation is the state of living together and having a sexual relationship without being married (Smock, 2000). It is an increasingly common phenomenon in modern society, particularly among younger adults. Cohabitation is an important concept in family science because it has significant implications for family formation and stability, as well as for individual well-being (DeRose et al., 2017).

Cohabitation can take many forms, ranging from a temporary arrangement to a long-term committed relationship. Some cohabiting couples may eventually get married, while others may choose to remain unmarried but still have a committed relationship. Cohabitation may also involve children from previous relationships or children born to the cohabiting couple.

Parenting Styles

The basic premise of the concept of parenting styles in family science is that different patterns of parenting behaviors have a significant impact on children's development and outcomes. Parenting styles are defined as "constellations of attitudes, behaviors, and strategies that parents use to interact with their children" (Baumrind, 1991, p. 62). Importantly, parenting styles should be understood and applied within context (Darling & Steinberg, 1993).

Authoritative
This style is characterized by high levels of warmth and responsiveness, coupled with high expectations for behavior and clear boundaries. Parents who use this style are communicative, flexible, and willing to listen to their children's opinions and feelings.

Authoritarian
This style is characterized by high levels of control and demands for obedience, with little warmth or responsiveness. Parents who use this style often have strict rules and expect their children to follow them without question.

Permissive
This style is characterized by high levels of warmth and responsiveness but low levels of control and discipline. Parents who use this style are indulgent and lenient, and may have difficulty enforcing rules or setting boundaries.

Neglectful

This style is characterized by low levels of both warmth and control, with little attention paid to children's needs or behavior. Parents who use this style may be absent or uninvolved in their children's lives.

Love Languages

The concept of love languages refers to the idea that individuals express and receive love in different ways. In the context of family science, the concept has been popularized by Gary Chapman (2010), who proposes that there are five love languages: words of affirmation, quality time, receiving gifts, acts of service, and physical touch. According to Chapman, understanding and speaking your partner's love language can improve the quality of your relationship and increase feelings of love and appreciation.

Each love language represents a different way of expressing affection and appreciation. Words of affirmation involve verbal compliments, praise, and encouragement. Quality time involves giving your partner your undivided attention and engaging in activities together. Receiving gifts involves giving thoughtful and meaningful presents as a symbol of love. Acts of service involve doing helpful and supportive things for your partner. Physical touch involves nonsexual physical contact, such as hugs, kisses, and holding hands.

Gottman's Four Horsemen

The Four Horsemen is a term coined by Julie and John Gottman (2017) to describe four communication patterns that are particularly destructive in marriage. These patterns are criticism, contempt, defensiveness, and stonewalling (Gottman & Silver, 2016).

Criticism involves attacking your partner's character or personality rather than focusing on a specific behavior or action. Contempt involves speaking to your partner with disrespect, sarcasm, or hostility. Defensiveness involves making excuses or blaming your partner when confronted with a problem or issue. Stonewalling involves withdrawing from the conversation or shutting down emotionally rather than engaging with your partner.

According to the Gottmans, these four communication patterns can lead to negative outcomes in marriage, including increased conflict, decreased satisfaction, and increased likelihood of divorce. However, they also suggest that couples can learn to recognize and avoid these patterns by developing better communication skills and practicing healthy conflict resolution.

Death and Dying in Family Relationships

The process of death and dying refers to the physical, emotional, and social changes that occur as a person approaches the end of their life. In family science, the process of death and dying is often studied in terms of the impact on the individual, their family members, and the broader community (Copp, 1998; Kübler-Ross, 2011; Kübler-Ross et al., 1972).

The process of death and dying typically involves several stages, which can vary depending on the individual and their circumstances. These stages may include shock and denial, anger, bargaining, depression, and acceptance. Throughout these stages, individuals may experience a range of physical and emotional symptoms, including pain, fatigue, anxiety, and sadness.

For family members and caregivers, the process of death and dying can also be emotionally challenging. They may experience grief, anxiety, and uncertainty, as well as a sense of loss and sadness. However, many families also report feeling a sense of closeness and connection during this time, as they come together to support their loved ones and each other.

Aging and Older Adulthood in Family Relationships

Aging and older adulthood refer to the physical, cognitive, and social changes that occur as individuals grow older. In family science, the study of aging and older adulthood focuses on the impact of these changes on individuals, families, and communities (Silverstein & Giarrusso, 2010).

As individuals age, they may experience a range of physical changes, including changes in sensory perception, decreased mobility, and increased risk of chronic illnesses. They may also experience changes in cognitive function, such as decreased memory and problem-solving abilities. These changes can impact daily activities and social interactions, and may require support from family members and caregivers.

In family science, the study of aging and older adulthood also considers the impact of these changes on families and communities. For example, family members may take on caregiving roles for aging relatives, which can impact their own physical, emotional, and financial well-being. Older adults may also face social isolation and exclusion, which can impact their mental health and well-being.

Overall, the study of aging and older adulthood in family science seeks to understand the complex interplay between individuals, families, and communities as they navigate the process of growing older (Bengtson & Settersten, 2016).

Moral Development in Family Relationships

Moral development refers to the process through which individuals acquire and internalize moral values, beliefs, and behaviors. In family science, the study of moral development focuses on the role of family and parenting practices in shaping children's moral development (Dunn, 2013; Grusec, 2019; Walker, 1999).

According to developmental psychologist Lawrence Kohlberg (1994), moral development progresses through a series of stages, each characterized by increasingly complex and abstract moral reasoning. At the earliest stage, children's moral reasoning is focused on avoiding punishment and satisfying their own needs. As they mature, children's moral reasoning becomes more focused on social norms and expectations, and eventually, on abstract principles of justice and morality.

Examples of moral development in children can include family communication and dialogue about moral issues, which is also important, as it allows children to develop their own moral reasoning skills and understand the perspectives of others.

Social Learning Theory

Important to effectively raising families is learning. The most obvious learning that occurs in families is parents' socialization of their children to help their young adapt to their social worlds. One of the main theories of human learning is called social learning theory. Social learning theory posits that individuals learn from observing and imitating others, as well as through reinforcement and punishment of behaviors. It emphasizes the role of environmental factors, such as social norms and modeling, in shaping behavior (Bandura & Walters, 1977). Children also socialize parents in a number of ways. For instance, children teach their parents about new technological advancements and social trends (O'Keeffe & Clarke-Pearson, 2011).

Eclectic Theoretical Orientation

The theories and frameworks addressed in this text are presented as individual theories. However, one of the leading approaches to the study of human and family development is an eclectic model approach, which allows scholars to take aspects of multiple theoretical perspectives to address some aspects of family life (Garfield & Kurtz, 1977). The eclectic theoretical orientation in family science involves drawing upon multiple theoretical perspectives and frameworks to understand and address family issues. Rather than adhering to a single theoretical approach, an eclectic orientation recognizes that different theories may be more or less effective depending on the specific situation or family.

References

Bandura, A., & Walters, R. H. (1977). *Social learning theory* (Vol. 1). Prentice-Hall.

Baumrind, D. (1991). The influence of parenting style on adolescent competence and substance use. *Journal of Early Adolescence*, *11*(1), 56–95. https://doi.org/10.1177/0272431691111004

Baxter, L. A. (1990). Dialectical contradictions in relationship development. *Journal of Social and Personal Relationships*, *7*(1), 69–88. https://doi.org/10.1177/0265407590071004

Baxter, L. A., Scharp, K. M., & Thomas, L. J. (2021). Relational dialectics theory. *Journal of Family Theory & Review*, *13*(1), 7–20. https://doi.org/10.1111/jftr.12405

Bengtson, V. L., & Settersten Jr, R. (Eds.). (2016). *Handbook of theories of aging*. Springer Publishing Company.

Chapman, G. D. (2010). *The 5 love languages: The secret to love that lasts*. Northfield Publishing.

Coleman, M., & Ganong, L. (1999). *Changing families, changing responsibilities: Family obligations following divorce and remarriage*. Psychology Press.

Copp, G. (1998). A review of current theories of death and dying. *Journal of Advanced Nursing*, *28*(2), 382–390. https://doi.org/10.1046/j.1365-2648.1998.00794.x

Darling, N., & Steinberg, L. (1993). Parenting style as context: An integrative model. *Psychological Bulletin*, *113*(3), 487–496. https://doi.org/10.1037/0033-2909.113.3.487

DeRose, L., Lyons-Amos, M., Wilcox, W., & Huarcaya, G. (2017). *The cohabitation go-round: Cohabitation and family instability across the globe*. Social Trends Institute.

Dunn, J. (2013). Moral development in early childhood and social interaction in the family. In M. Killen & J. G. Smetana (Eds.), *Handbook of moral development* (pp. 135–159). Psychology Press.

Erikson, E. H. (1974). *Identity and the life cycle* (reissue ed.). W. W. Norton.

Fine, M. A., & Harvey, J. H. (Eds.). (2013). *Handbook of divorce and relationship dissolution*. Psychology Press.

Garfield, S. L., & Kurtz, R. (1977). A study of eclectic views. *Journal of Consulting and Clinical Psychology*, *45*(1), 78. https://psycnet.apa.org/doi/10.1037/0022-006X.45.1.78

Gottman, J., & Gottman, J. (2017). The natural principles of love. *Journal of Family Theory & Review*, *9*(1), 7–26. https://doi.org/10.1111/jftr.12182

Gottman, J., & Silver, N. (2016). *The seven principles for making marriage work: A practical guide from the country's foremost relationship expert*. Harmony.

Graham, J. M., Liu, Y. J., & Jeziorski, J. L. (2006). The dyadic adjustment scale: A reliability generalization meta-analysis. *Journal of Marriage and Family*, *68*(3), 701–717. https://doi.org/10.1111/j.1741-3737.2006.00284.x

Grusec, J. E. (2019). *The Oxford handbook of parenting and moral development*. Oxford University Press.

Guzzo, K. B. (2014). New partners, more kids: Multiple-partner fertility in the United States. *The Annals of the American Academy of Political and Social Science*, *654*(1), 66–86. https://doi.org/10.1177/0002716214525571

Jones, J., Rodger, S., Walpole, A., & Bobir, N. (2019). Holding the cards: Empowering families through an ASD family goal setting tool. *Topics in Early Childhood Special Education*, *39*(2), 117–130. https://doi.org/10.1177/0271121418766240

James, A. G. (2023). *Family goal setting: A practical guide*. Prof_Ajames Enterprises.

Kohlberg, L. (1994). *Moral development: Kohlberg's original study of moral development* (No. 3). Taylor & Francis.

Kübler-Ross, E. (2011). *Living with death and dying*. Simon and Schuster.

Kübler-Ross, E., Wessler, S., & Avioli, L. V. (1972). On death and dying. *Jama*, *221*(2), 174–179.

McAdams, D. P. (2004). Generativity and the narrative ecology of family life. In M. W. Pratt & B. H. Fiese (Eds.), *Family stories and the life course* (pp. 249–272). Routledge.

Monte, L. M. (2019). Multiple-partner fertility in the United States: A demographic portrait. *Demography*, *56*(1), 103–127. https://doi.org/10.1007/s13524-018-0743-y

Moore, T. J., & Asay, S. M. (2017). *Family resource management*. SAGE Publications.

O'Keeffe, G. S., & Clarke-Pearson, K. (2011). The impact of social media on children, adolescents, and families. *Pediatrics*, *127*(4), 800–804. https://doi.org/10.1542/peds.2011-0054

Rodger, S., O'Keefe, A., Cook, M., & Jones, J. (2012). Parents' and service providers' perceptions of the family goal setting tool: A pilot study. *Journal of Applied Research in Intellectual Disabilities*, *25*(4), 360–371. https://doi.org/10.1111/j.1468-3148.2011.00674.x

Silverstein, M., & Giarrusso, R. (2010). Aging and family life: A decade review. *Journal of Marriage and Family*, *72*(5), 1039–1058. https://doi.org/10.1111/j.1741-3737.2010.00749.x

Smock, P. J. (2000). Cohabitation in the United States: An appraisal of research themes, findings, and implications. *Annual Review of Sociology*, *26*(1), 1–20. https://doi.org/10.1146/annurev.soc.26.1.1

Spanier, G. B. (1989). *Dyadic adjustment scale*. Multi-Health Systems.

Sussman, M. B., Steinmetz, S. K., & Peterson, G. W. (Eds.). (2013). *Handbook of marriage and the family*. Springer Science & Business Media.

Walker, L. J. (1999). The family context for moral development. *Journal of Moral Education*, *28*(3), 261–264.

Conclusion

The study and application of major family theories can play a crucial role in promoting healthy family functioning. This book has explored several theories, including attachment theory, family systems theory, social exchange theory, and ecological systems theory, along with some relevant theories of human development, such as the relational developmental systems model, to help explain how individuals (human individuals) and family members develop.

Each of these theories offers a unique perspective on family dynamics and functioning, and can help professionals who study and work with families to better understand the complexities of human relationships. By using multiple theories to study and engage with families, professionals can gain a more nuanced understanding of family dynamics and be better equipped to promote positive change.

Throughout this book, I have emphasized the importance of applying these theories in context. Families are diverse and complex, and no single theory can fully capture the experiences and needs of all families. By using an eclectic theoretical orientation, professionals can tailor their approach to each family's unique needs and circumstances.

In addition, this book has emphasized the importance of using these theories to promote healthy family functioning. Whether through prevention or intervention, professionals who work with families have a critical role to play in promoting positive outcomes for individuals and families alike. By understanding the theories that underpin healthy family functioning, professionals can be better equipped to promote positive change in families and contribute to the well-being of individuals and communities as a whole.

Overall, this book has provided a comprehensive [introductory] guide to major family theories and their application in promoting healthy family functioning. By combining theoretical knowledge with practical skills, professionals who study and work with families can help to create positive change and build stronger, healthier, and more resilient families.

Index